COMPLETE PLAYS

Other Books by Ronald Firbank

Vainglory (1915)
Inclinations (1916)
Caprice (1917)
Valmouth (1919)
Santal (1921)
The Flower beneath the Foot (1923)
Prancing Nigger (1924)
Concerning the Eccentricities of Cardinal Pirelli (1926)
The Artificial Princess (1934)
The New Rythum and Other Pieces (1962)
Complete Short Stories (1990)

RONALD FIRBANK

COMPLETE PLAYS

Edited with an Introduction by
Steven Moore

Dalkey Archive Press

The Mauve Tower and *A Disciple from the Country* were first published in 1991 by Quartet Books (London) in *The Early Firbank,* edited by Steven Moore. ©1991, 1994 by Thomas Firbank.

The Princess Zoubaroff was originally published in 1920 by Grant Richards (London) and is now in the Public Domain.

Introduction, arrangement, and textual notes ©1994 by Dalkey Archive Press.

First Edition, June 1994

Library of Congress Cataloging-in-Publication Data
Firbank, Ronald, 1886-1926.
[Plays]
Complete plays / Ronald Firbank ; edited with an introduction by Steven Moore.
— 1st ed.
Contents: The mauve tower — A disciple from the country — The Princess Zoubaroff.
I. Moore, Steven, 1951-   . II. Title.
PR6011.I7A19   1994   822'.912—dc20   93-36133

Partially funded by grants from the National Endowment for the Arts and the Illinois Arts Council.

Dalkey Archive Press
4241 Illinois State University
Normal, IL 61790-4241

Printed on permanent/durable acid-free paper and bound in the United States of America

CONTENTS

Introduction

The drama and the novel have enough similarities that most novelists try their hand at a play sometime in their career, just as many playwrights attempt a novel at some point. For most novelists, their plays occupy a minor place in their oeuvre—Henry James's plays and Joyce's *Exiles* are convenient examples—just as the novels of playwrights are often mere footnotes in their careers (like Shaw's *The Irrational Knot* or Coward's *Pomp and Circumstance*). Writers who excel in both genres are rare— Beckett and Genet, maybe Duras if you include filmscripts—and while Firbank's achievement in theater is secondary to that in the novel, the drama played a significant role in his development as an artist.

From an early age, Firbank was enamored of the theater. As a boy he collected autographs of playwrights and actors, and by the time he was fifteen he was attending such plays as Daudet's *Sapho* and Pinero's *Iris*. A few years later, in 1904, Firbank moved to Paris, where opportunities for attending plays and meeting actors were plentiful. Ostensibly there to perfect his French, Firbank spent as much time cultivating his personality, and he took many of his cues from Parisian theater life. In her biography of Firbank, Miriam Benkovitz details some of his enthusiasms:

Theater and theatrical personalities, of course, delighted Firbank. He watched eagerly for the bills, green for the Opéra-Comique and wine-red for the Comédie-Française, posted to announce new productions. It was the green which he read more eagerly: the Opéra-Comique never failed to please, and operettas—*La Chauve Souris,* for example—were most amusing. His admiration for La Belle Otéro was devout; he went again and again to the Mathurins to see her in the pantomime *Rêve d'Opium* or in M. Gailhard's *L'Aragonaise*, and he filled pages of his photographic album with her pictures. He sat entranced before Polaire as Fiquet in Willy's *Claudine à Paris* as well as before his old favorites. Réjane was at the Théâtre de Variété; and the Divine Sarah created the part of Marie Antoinette in *Varenne,* which opened on April 23 [1904], and re-created Aiglon for twenty performances commencing on October 1. He went through the stage door to visit Mlle Jeanne Granier and Édouard de Max, who was at the Théâtre Sarah Bernhardt or the Théâtre Porte-Saint-Martin.[1]

This Rumanian actor, "reputed to have a bad influence on young men" (Benkovitz reports), became friendly with the English teenager and added a decadent dimension to Firbank's budding dandyism. At the time, Firbank was reading the Symbolists, the Pre-Raphaelites, Maurice Maeterlinck, and, most importantly, Oscar Wilde. It was in this heady atmosphere that Firbank wrote his first play, *The Mauve Tower,* dated in the dedication the summer of 1904. (The dedication on the typescript reads: "A Monsieur Jean Pozzi / Très cordialement je dédie ma 'Tour Mauve' en souvenir de l'été mil neuf cent quatre": Pozzi was a slightly older. friend of the family Firbank was staying with.) Like some of the prose pieces Firbank wrote that year— "La Princesse aux Soleils," "Far Away," "Harmonie" (all of which appear in the *Complete Short Stories*)—the play is more concerned with setting and description than with narrative or characterization. Firbank here is like a young artist more interested in exploring the colors on his palette than with painting something substantial, or a musician experimenting with chords and tonalities. The young writer can be seen testing his metaphor-making abilities ("the moon looks like a yellow jewel, like a strange yellow jewel from some dead king's crown") and paying homage, through imitation, to important influences like Maeterlinck's plays, Wilde's *Salomé,* and, perhaps, Debussy's *Pelléas et Mélisande.* It's a derivative, juvenile effort, and yet a major theme of Firbank's later work—alienation—is present here in the circumstances of the Princess Ingria fleeing from an unwanted marriage and the Prince Laon's wrongful imprisonment by his uncles. Neither is integrated into his or her society, a situation shared by many of Firbank's characters.

---

[1]Miriam J. Benkovitz, *Ronald Firbank: A Biography* (New York: Knopf, 1969), 47.

Introduction

If *The Mauve Tower* recalls Wilde's *Salomé*, Firbank's next play, *A Disciple from the Country*, recalls Wilde's comedies. Firbank wrote this play three years later at Cambridge University. In 1907 he joined two of the university's dramatic societies—the Amateur Dramatic Club and the Footlights—and Benkovitz suggests he wrote this play some time that year in lieu of participating in performances. Brigid Brophy, in her spirited biography of Firbank, refines the date further to argue he wrote it before May of 1907, the month Richard Strauss's opera version of Wilde's *Salomé* premiered in Paris;[2] hence Mrs. Creamway's observation (on Mary Magdalen's alleged engagement to John the Baptist): "They tell me the whole thing has been turned quite recently into a very tuneful opera."

In style, content, and dramatic technique, *A Disciple from the Country* is completely opposite to, and a marked improvement upon, *The Mauve Tower*. Alan Hollinghurst has noted that all of Firbank's juvenilia falls into two categories: those he wrote for his mother and those written about her.[3] "Baba," as her son called Lady Firbank, doted on his impressionistic prose poems and pastels in prose, of which *The Mauve Tower* is a florid example. But from an early age Firbank also began writing satirical stories about characters like Lady Firbank and her social set. Such early stories as "When Widows Love," "Her Dearest Friend," and "A Tragedy in Green" show Firbank's first, tentative lashes of the whip of satire, at which he would grow murderously proficient in later works. The triviality of Mayfair social life, especially when combined with religiosity, is a subject that Firbank would return in his later novels, and this early play shows how natural the satirical impulse came to him.

The play has a variety of connections with Firbank's other work of the same period. Lady Seafairer suggests that Stella's marriage to a bishop would allow her the opportunity to erect a cathedral window to herself; this same ambition is shared by Lady Henrietta Worthing in his story "A

[2]Brigid Brophy, *Prancing Novelist: A Defence of Fiction in the Form of a Critical Biography in Praise of Ronald Firbank* (London: Macmillan, 1973), 316.

[3]Alan Hollinghurst, "Introduction," *The Early Firbank,* ed. Steven Moore (London: Quartet, 1991), ix.

Study in Opal," written the same year (1907). (Mrs. Creamway's allegedly haunted house in St Catherine-in-the-Marsh is Lady Henrietta's residence as well.) Lord George Blueharnis's name is merely a syllable away from Lady Georgia Blueharnis's in "A Tragedy in Green," another story written about the same time, which also refers to a Jane Seafairer, though it's impossible to tell if this is the Lady Seafairer of the play.

Neither of these plays was published or performed in Firbank's lifetime. Indeed, when he came across them in 1925 amongst his papers, he wrote "Not to be published" on both of them. He did, however, draw upon *A Disciple* for his later works. Mary Magdalen's alleged engagement to John the Baptist is repeated in chapter 13 of *Vainglory,* Firbank's first published novel (1915), in which Lady Georgia Blueharnis reappears. Stella Creamway's ambition to marry a bishop and erect a church window to herself provides the basic plot of the same novel.

In the years after he went down from Cambridge, Firbank continued to attend plays and ballets, both in England and abroad. One of his early novels, the wonderful *Caprice* (1917), treats theater life in London with bemused affection, and that novel even tries out a memorable stage direction later used in his next and final play, *The Princess Zoubaroff.* (In chap. 13 of the novel, a young man is described as having "a voice like cheap scent," used in act 1, scene 11 of the play to described Reggie Quintus's voice.) *The Princess Zoubaroff* falls into a different category than the two earlier plays, for it was published in Firbank's lifetime (though it wouldn't be performed for decades after) and is usually counted among his mature works. He wrote the play in London in 1919-20 and published it between his fourth and fifth novels (i.e., *Valmouth,* 1919, and *Santal,* 1921). As with his novels, Firbank constructed the play from lines written in notebooks, and then crossed out as he found a place for them in the work at hand. Two surviving notebooks for *The Princess Zoubaroff* offer many examples of lines not used (nor ascribed to any character):

Humour is a weapon that needs sharpening every day.

In England people are so moral they would arrest the Moon for following the Sun—

Pere Puget used to say I made epigrams even at Confession—They would come!

I'm fairly hardened. Ever since I was a child I was talked about.

One finds her now more often than not on her knees.

Just now she was malicious enough to openly condole.

Poor soul! Soured by six seasons! . . .

You feel like after a dose of chloral, an intense absolute lethargy, that's quite overwhelmingly delicious.

She is too healthy to love with passion.

Reading us a paper on corporeal charm v. mental fascination.

He's witty and insinuating, your husband I find.

Ah well—I suppose in the end, we shall all be reduced to living on our own estates—

Conceited creature!

His temperament is an enigma.

It's all an enigma.

Horridly artful.

The charmingest man.[4]

The book was published in November 1920 in a small edition of 530 copies, and illustrated with two drawings by Michel Sevier (reproduced on the jacket of the present edition.) The reviews, like most of those Firbank received for his novels, were unsympathetic. The *Times Literary Supplement* gave it a brief, lukewarm notice criticizing the lack of dramatic development, the inadequate plot, and Firbank's "curious adventures in spelling." The *Spectator* said "There is something vaguely unpleasant in its *fin de siècle* attitude," but admitted Firbank had "an extraordinary knack of

---

[4]From the sale catalog of Swann Galleries, New York, Sale Number 1421, December 11, 1986, item no. 249. These two notebooks were formerly in the possession of Miriam Benkovitz; their present whereabouts is unknown.

writing dialogue, and his entirely odious people move and breathe and are completely real." Firbank naturally wanted to see his play staged and the following year discussed this with actress Lillah McCarthy; she expressed interest, but efforts to finance the play failed. He told Sewell Stokes that he sent the play to Charles B. Cochran to read, as well as to "*all* my favourite actresses," but nothing came of his efforts.

When the play finally received its first staging, in June 1951 at the Watergate Theatre in London, it met with a different reception. The *Times* reviewer was delighted with it, finding it "twice as amusing" to watch than to read. The play was also staged in 1952 at the Irving Theatre in London and in 1975 at the Tower Theatre, Islington. A radio adaptation by Archie Campbell was broadcast on the BBC's Third Programme in 1962, with Dame Edith Evans in the title role. Jonathan Kent, one of the directors of the Almeida Theatre, also in Islington, wanted to produce the play during the 1991 Christmas season, but a financial crisis forced him to shelve the idea.

Reading the play today, it's inconceivable that it could have been staged in Firbank's own day. It is one of his most unapologetically homosexual works, and one can only wonder how even a sophisticated British audience would have reacted to the openly gay and lesbian flirting in some scenes (Reggie with Angelo in act 2, scene 11; the Princess with Enid in act 1, scene 7, and again in act 2, scene 4), or to Reggie dancing at the end of act 2 with a newly published poet named Astix ("a wild young man who looks like the Publishers' Ruin"), or indeed to the ongoing argument for homosexual separatism that develops over the course of the play. The institution of marriage is mocked throughout, motherhood is seen as a calamity (Nadine's pregnancy is likened to the Plague), and in one of his most daring moves, Firbank aligns lesbianism with purity and the religious life, consigning heterosexuality to the profane world.

The play has such a light, inconsequential air about it that it is not apparent at first how radical a critique of conventional standards this work is. Even Firbank's later critics have steered clear of the play, either ignoring it altogther or dismissing it as a minor, unsuccessful work. Brigid Brophy is, of course, an exception and devotes two dozen brilliant pages to this work.[5] Among other things, she notes that not only does the relationship between Lord Henry Orkish and Reggie Quintus evoke that of Oscar Wilde and Bosie Douglas, but that Reggie is an alter ego for Firbank himself, allowing the play to function as a kind of dream date between Firbank and his martyred master. Firbank reverses Wilde's unhappy fate by showing him happily in exile, a fantasy of how things might have turned out for Wilde had England held the liberal, humane view of homosexuality displayed in *The Princess Zoubaroff.*

---

[5]See *Prancing Novelist,* 195-99, 326-34, and 486-99. The only other critic who has discussed *The Princess Zoubaroff* at length is Parker Tyler; see his essay "The Prince Zoubaroff: Praise of Ronald Firbank," *Prose* 2 (1971): 155-69.

THE MAUVE TOWER

A DREAM PLAY IN VII SCENES

PERSONS IN THE PLAY

THE PRINCESS INGRIA
LIERIES, *her slave*
THE PRINCE LAON
THREE SHADOWS
A SENTINEL

THE SCENES

A forest of palm trees, through which the distant sea is seen. It is night.

Enter the PRINCESS INGRIA *and* LIERIES *her slave. The* PRINCESS *wears a robe of blue-green gauze embroidered with silver flowers.*

In her hair black and white ostrich feathers are fastened to a pale red veil.

Her hair falls to her feet and is plaited with rubies and strange mauve stones. As she walks the stones jingle, and her veil floats behind her like a sail. LIERIES *the slave wears a robe of orange and red, a leopard skin is thrown across her shoulders and in her blue-black hair a white lily is fastened; her arms and neck are covered with heavy gold ornaments, in her hands she carries a silver harp inlaid with sapphires.*

THE PRINCESS INGRIA [*singing*]: Oh! how beautiful is the night! how wonderful is the night! how gold the stars!

LIERIES [*glancing around her*]: Hush! Hush, do not sing so loud.

INGRIA: Oh! Oh! the moon, do you see the moon? It is like a full blown flower, it is like a yellow rose, through the palm trees it looks like a yellow rose.

LIERIES [*glancing around her*]: Hush, hush, do not sing so loud.

INGRIA: Oh! hark! hark! the birds! do you hear the birds? All the forest is alive with birds, never, never, was a wood so full of birds. See, see, in the big blue palms the birds of Paradise. . . . Their tails are like showers of falling gold. . . . Lieries, oh! Lieries look at the butterflies, all the air is silver with the butterflies.

LIERIES [*glancing around*]: Hush, hush, do not sing so loud.

INGRIA: Oh! Oh! the flowers! do you smell the flowers? All the forest is

3

perfumed with the flowers. They look like dragons' eyes peering at us through the dark. The scarlet lilies look like bleeding wounds. The great white orchids look like hands. The yellow grasses look like golden swords.

LIERIES: Hush, hush, I am afraid.

INGRIA: Why are you afraid? What makes you afraid?

LIERIES: I do not know.

INGRIA: Oh! the sea, the sea, the moon is disappearing into the sea; the moon looks like a yellow jewel, like a strange yellow jewel from some dead king's crown. All the stars are falling into the sea, it is like a shower of silver flowers.

LIERIES: I see strange pictures in the moon.

INGRIA: What do you see?

LIERIES [*hiding her face in her hands*]: I am afraid.

INGRIA: The sea looks like a yellow fire, like a sheet of yellow flame. . . . Listen! how still it is . . . the birds have ceased to sing. . . . All the palm trees are trembling, and yet there is no wind. Never before have I felt a night so hot. Oh! how dark it is, I cannot see the flowers, I can no longer see the moon. Lieries, Lieries, I cannot see you, Oh! Oh! I am afraid.

LIERIES: Something terrible is going to happen.

INGRIA: Where are we? Where can we be?

LIERIES: I do not know.

[*Curtain, music plays softly*]

SCENE II

The seashore. It is still very dark. Enter INGRIA *and* LIERIES; *they walk hand in hand.* INGRIA *leads the way.*

INGRIA: Where are we?

LIERIES: I can hear the sea.

INGRIA: Take care, take care, do not walk into the sea.

LIERIES: The sea is very calm, it does not move, the water is so still that it might be dead.

INGRIA: The sea is dead?

LIERIES: I can see a line of crimson in the east, it will soon be light.

INGRIA: Let us sit down on the sands and wait.

LIERIES: Wait for what?

INGRIA: The day.

[*They sit down silently and watch the dawn creeping up over the sea.*]

LIERIES: I can smell oranges.

INGRIA [*glancing around*]: There is a wood of oranges growing on the seashore.

LIERIES: I have never heard of orange trees growing on the seashore.

INGRIA: There are also palm trees and pomegranates, all along the seacoast grow strange white flowers that look like priests. . . . And through the palm trees I can see a tall mauve tower.

LIERIES: It is perhaps a mosque.

INGRIA: No, no, it is not a mosque.

LIERIES: How do you know?

INGRIA: It is a palace, I can see the sentinels on the tower.

LIERIES: Oh! I am afraid, let us be gone.

INGRIA: No, no we will go to the palace and ask to see the Sultan.

LIERIES: I think you are mad.

INGRIA: We cannot always live upon the seashore.

LIERIES: Oh! Princess, Princess, return to your father's palace, I pray of you to return to your father's palace.

INGRIA: We are lost, you know very well that we are lost, and besides I will never marry the Prince Tegia, I would sooner die.

[*Day suddenly dawns.*]

LIERIES [*stretching out her arms in ecstasy towards the sun*]: Oh! the sun! the sun! this must be the country of the sun. The blue sea is turning yellow in the sun.

INGRIA [*in rapture looking around her*]: There are snow mountains! See, see there are snow mountains. They look like marble temples against the sky.

LIERIES: And the desert seems to stretch away to the end of the world.

INGRIA: I can see camels on the desert, a long chain of camels going slowly towards the sun.

LIERIES: Look at our shadows upon the golden sand. The earth is like a mirror, like a great yellow mirror, oh the sun! the sun! [*She falls on her knees her face towards the sun.*]

INGRIA [*smiling with happiness*]: Oh! see the town is like a garden of flowers. All the streets are lined with palm trees, and the houses are dazzling white. . . . The towers of the mosques are green and rose, and there is a great mauve tower like an iris that stands upon a hill. . . . There are gardens on the housetops all ablaze with flowers. Oh! Oh! they are all sunflowers, some of them are bright red, others orange. . . . They look like giants against the sky. And the palace is all white, as if it were covered in snow, on the roofs are gardens of palm trees, and marble fountains throw water high into the air like silver plumes.

LIERIES: Oh! the sun! the sun!

INGRIA: Come, we will go to the palace and ask to see the Sultan.

LIERIES: Where can we be? In whose country can we be?

INGRIA [*speaking very slowly*]: I think we are in the country of the sun.

[*Curtain, music plays softly*]

SCENE III

Before the palace gates.

The gateposts are of red and white marble. From the gateposts hangs a great gold door curiously carved. Through the door can be seen a court full of palm trees. In the centre of the court stands an obelisk of black marble inlaid with gold. In the trees sing many wonderfully coloured birds. Under the palm trees are fountains of green and white mosaic that throw water up amidst the leaves. There is no one to be seen in the court, all is perfectly silent, except for the song of the birds and the splash of the water in the fountains. At the end of the garden can be seen the mauve tower clearly silhouetted against a blazing sky. Before the palace gates a black sentry walks languidly to and fro.

Enter INGRIA *and* LIERIES. INGRIA *holds a bunch of lotus flowers in her hands, her face is hidden by her veil.*

6

INGRIA [*to the* SENTINEL]: Who is the Sultan of this town?

THE SENTINEL: Who are you?

INGRIA: I will not say.

LIERIES: My mistress wishes to speak with the Sultan.

THE SENTINEL: That is impossible.

INGRIA: Why? Why impossible.

THE SENTINEL: The Sultan is mad.

LIERIES [*to* INGRIA]: Let us be gone, let us be gone.

INGRIA: No, I will not go, I wish to see the Sultan.

LIERIES: Why do you wish to see the Sultan?

INGRIA: I do not know.

LIERIES: Come, come, mistress this is folly; let us be gone, let us go now at once.

INGRIA: No, I will not go. [*To* THE SENTINEL:] See now I will give you this chain of rubies, if you will let me pass the gates.

THE SENTINEL: I dare not for it would mean my life.

INGRIA: Yes, yes, you will let me pass and I will give you this necklace of pale mauve stones. I will give you also my silver fan. I will give you my silver fan that was taken from the tomb of a dead queen of Egypt. It was found in a strangely painted vault in the heart of a pyramid. These mauve stones too were found amidst her hair. No one knows what stones they are, no one knows how old they are, probably they are older than the world.

THE SENTINEL: Who are you? Who are you?

INGRIA: I will not say.

THE SENTINEL [*staring at her*]: Are you some goddess, for if so, then will I let you pass. For twelve long years now our Sultan has been mad. Never does he leave the palace gates. They say he worships the sun, that all day he talks and whispers with the sun. Sometimes, it is true, I have seen him myself on the tall mauve tower, his arms outstretched towards the sun. Strange tales were told by prophets at his birth. Strange things take place within the palace walls. All the town is whispering about the mauve tower, at night the people collect beneath the palm trees, and sit silently watching the mauve tower. Something terrible is going to happen. Something terrible is going to take place. Ever since the last moon a great black bird has hovered about the tower. Ah! ah! the wings of death hover over the town.

INGRIA: Let me pass, let me pass.

THE SENTINEL: Show me your face, first show me your face.

[INGRIA *lifts aside her veil, the* SENTINEL *stares at her a moment, then falls at her feet hiding his face in his hands.*]

INGRIA: Come Lieries. [*She walks slowly through the golden gate, followed by* LIERIES, *who now begins to play softly on her harp. The birds in the trees burst into an ecstasy of song. A quantity of silver butterflies hover around the harp as* LIERIES *plays, they seem to be fascinated by the sound. . . . In a fountain of red and black marble grow a quantity of tall green lilies. All the air smells of roses, and about the trunks of the palm trees cling mysterious-looking orchids.* INGRIA *walks as in a dream, her eyes fixed upon the mauve tower, at the foot of the tower she stops. A purple curtain hangs across the door, the curtain is embroidered with sunflowers, prophets, and strange birds.* INGRIA *pulls the curtain timidly aside, and reveals a great silver idol. Before the idol a quantity of flowers are burning as sacrifice—all the flowers are mauve.* INGRIA *stands a moment motionless in the doorway, then making a sign to* LIERIES *not to follow her she disappears.* LIERIES *hovers a moment hesitating on the threshold, suddenly she hears the sound of wings in the air, she looks above her, and there hanging motionless above the mauve tower is a great black bird.*]

LIERIES [*covering her face in her hands*]: Oh! I am afraid. I am afraid.

[*Curtain, music plays softly*]

SCENE IV

A staircase in the mauve tower.

A flight of mauve marble stairs that seem to lead away into the sky. The walls are mauve mosaic. From the walls hang enormous shields and spears, on the shields are painted pictures of idols surrounded with flowers. The staircase twists about in an unaccountable manner. Through a tall narrow window covered with a mauve curtain shines the sun. All the air is mauve, through a small window however, in the shape of a star, can be seen the distant sea, by this window the sun pours in a great bar of golden light. As the curtain rises the PRINCESS INGRIA *is seen listening on the staircase. Her back is to the audience and she is halfway up the flight of stairs that leads to the star window. Her long green robe curls behind her like a serpent's tail, she fans herself with her silver fan as she moves, then arriving at the star window she stops.*]

INGRIA [*listening*]: No, I hear no one. I can hear nothing. These stairs seem to lead away to nowhere. [*She looks about her.*] Ah! here is a window. [*She stands on tiptoe and looks out, then gives a little cry.*] Ah! how high I am, I am right up amidst the blue, never in all my life have I been so high. [*She leans out a little.*] I am still in the mauve tower, far below me I see the birds fluttering like jewels amidst the trees, I can see Lieries, she is sitting on the edge of a fountain, she is playing on her harp, and she is looking at herself as she plays, in the clear water. Oh! oh! but she cannot see herself for all the water is covered with yellow flowers. There are a lot of silver butterflies clinging about the tower. Oh! Oh! all the mauve tower is covered with silver butterflies. At the foot of the tower is a lake, I can see the reflection of the mauve tower in the lake, it looks like a great dragon sleeping at the bottom of the clear water. Ah! ah! and I can see myself as I stand here in the window, like a little flower, all reflected in the green lake. And above, above, oh! I see a man's face, he is standing at the window looking at me, [*something splashes in the lake*] oh! something has moved in the lake, I can see nothing now. [*She climbs down from the window.*] I am afraid, I am afraid.

[*She stands listening, in her fright she lets fall all her lotus flowers also her silver fan. Suddenly steps are heard as of someone descending the staircase. The* PRINCESS *gives a little cry and commences running down stairs. She disappears. There is a pause. Steps are heard descending, then a young man, a drawn sword in his hands passes quickly across the scene, as he runs he treads upon the silver fan of the* PRINCESS, *he turns, looks at it, picks it up, then with the silver fan in one hand and the drawn sword in the other, he disappears on the winding mauve staircase, by which the* PRINCESS INGRIA *has passed.*]

[*Curtain, music plays softly*]

SCENE V

A corridor. The walls are blue and are painted with sunflowers and idols, a curtain hangs across a corner of the passage. Enter the PRINCESS INGRIA *running.*

INGRIA: He is following me, he is following me, oh why did I come? [*She runs to the end of the scene and finds there is no door.*] I am caught, I cannot get out there is no door. [*She stands still trembling her back against the wall.*] I will wait for him here. [*The steps are heard growing nearer, and nearer.*] Oh! if he should kill me!

[*Suddenly she catches sight of her harp that hangs at her waist, she unfastens it rapidly and in a low sweet voice begins to sing, accompanying herself with the harp. There is a pause, then in the open doorway a man appears, he walks slowly as in a dream, in one of his hands he holds a long gold sword that glitters with enormous jewels, and in the other a little silver fan. He is very beautiful and as the* PRINCESS *gazes at him her voice becomes fainter and fainter.*]

THE MAN: Who are you, what are you doing here?

INGRIA: I am the Princess Ingria.

THE MAN: The Princess Ingria? I have never heard of you before.

INGRIA: No, no, I am sure you have not. I come from a distant country very, very far from here, my father wished me to marry the Prince Tegia, but I would not, no, no, I would not. So I escaped from my father's palace with my slave, and we wandered for many days, through great forests where the trees were so thick that we could not see the sun. Then at sundown yesterday, we came upon the sea. We saw the moon peering through the palm trees like a pale face. We saw the stars falling through the sky. Strange birds were in the trees, and all the wood was carpeted with great white flowers.

THE MAN: How beautiful you are. [*A long silence.*]

INGRIA: Who are you?

THE MAN: I am the Prince Laon, by right Sultan of this land. My mother and father died when I was very young, and I was left in the care of three

10

uncles, who now rule my country. When I was a boy I used to kneel in worship to the sun, and my uncles wishing to kill me, or keep me from my rights, declared that I was mad, and had me imprisoned in this high mauve tower.

INGRIA: But you are not mad, you are as sane as I. I thought you were a god when you first entered by this door.

LAON: And I, I thought you were a pale goddess from the moon! for upon the staircase in the mauve tower, I found this little silver fan, embroidered in white pearls with crowns and crescent moons.

INGRIA [*smiling*]: It is mine, [*then sorrowfully*] it was given me by my mother when she died.

LAON: Oh! how beautiful your eyes are when they cloud with tears. Your eyes are like two blue flowers, like two blue flowers after rain.

INGRIA: Oh! how sweet your voice sounds when you speak, it is like a distant harp, it sounds like a harp played far away upon the seashore.

LAON: Hush! hush, below us in the garden all the birds are singing, but there is not one bird, there is not one bird amidst all the trees, that has a voice as sweet as yours.

INGRIA: Let us go into the garden, and I will sing to you. We will sit by the side of the lake under the shade of a palm tree, and we will watch the shadows of the birds as they fly amongst the flowers.

[*As she speaks a man's shadow is seen to pass quickly from behind a curtain, and disappear noiselessly on to the staircase.*]

LAON [*his hand on his sword*]: Who passed?

INGRIA: I saw a shadow.

LAON [*bursting forth*]: Ah! Ah! you do not know what it is. I live in daily terror for my life. At night I dare not sleep, for fear, for fear . . .

INGRIA [*taking his hand*]: For fear of what?

LAON [*whispering, as if he were dreaming*]: One night I fell asleep upon the tower. I dreamt that I was sailing on the sea in a great gold ship with purple-coloured sails. Behind me in the water trailed strange silks. From the sky fell a quantity of stars, and far away above the tall mauve tower hung the round white moon. Upon the distant shore the birds were singing in the trees, and the long pale sands shone dimly like dead gold. On the

11

deck were many silver cages full of doves, and now and then a slave would let one fly, and it would skim across the sea, cooing softly towards the woods. I thought I heard strange music in the air—strange instruments of music—then a voice, it sang the same sweet song that you just now sang. It was so sweet that I thought that I was dead. Then with a start I awoke. Three black forms were standing over me, and in the pale moonlight I saw the gleam of knives.

INGRIA [*trembling*]: Oh! Oh! I am afraid.

LAON [*taking her by the hand*]: Come, we will go and watch the sun shining upon the sea.

[*Curtain, music plays softly*]

SCENE VI

A garden by the lake. Through the palm trees can be seen the sea. In the lake the mauve tower is reflected, and by the lakeside kneel LAON *and* INGRIA, *they peer down through the water as if they are looking for something.*

INGRIA: I have never seen such beautiful fishes, I have never seen such wonderful fishes.

LAON: They have been there many hundreds of years.

INGRIA [*leaning over almost into the water*]: How beautiful to live at the bottom of the clear water, to live under the leaf of a white flower.

LAON: Take care Ingria do not lean so far into the water, oh! oh! your red veil has fallen into the lake.

INGRIA [*laughing*]: Ah! Ah! see how the fishes are frightened, they swim away and hide themselves beneath the flowers.

LAON: Far away I can hear the ringing of the temple bells, it must be evening. [*A long silence.*]

INGRIA: Ah! see! see! a yellow fish!

[LAON *bends over her, and they both gaze into the water but* LAON *only sees the reflection of* INGRIA's *face in the green lake.*]

12

LAON: I only see your face. Your face is reflected in all the lake. Your pale face surrounded with an aureole of silver butterflies.

INGRIA [*smiling*]: And I see you too, you too are reflected in the lake, your gold robe looks like the shining sun. Ah! Ah! give me your sword, give me your sword. [*She peers down through the water.*]

LAON [*giving her his sword*]: What do you see in the water?

INGRIA: A big grey fish, it caught two little silver fish, Ah! Ah! Ah! Ah! [*She splashes the water with the sword.*]

LAON: Take care, take care you will fall into the water.

INGRIA: Oh! oh! the grey fish has killed the two little silver fish!

LAON: Come, come we will go and listen to the birds singing amongst the roses.

INGRIA: Yes, yes, we will go and make chains of roses, and hang them in the trees. And I will sing to you. I will sing to you a song so sad, that you will weep!

[*They wander slowly away through the trees, the sky suddenly flushes crimson, and far away a bell rings sadly as if it were tolling for someone dead. Then the shadows begin to creep over the garden, long blue shadows that grow longer every instant. In the trees the birds sing drowsily, and the water in the fountains splashes monotonously. The lake changes to the colour of the sky—orange and red. The reflection of the mauve tower trembles incessantly as a bird skims across the lake touching the water with its wings. Then far away a harp is heard, then the voice of* INGRIA *singing very slowly a song infinitely sad. She ceases.*

A great silence falls upon the garden, only broken by the distant tolling of a silver bell.

Amongst the long grasses, and purple irises by the lakeside, lies the forgotten sword.]

[*Curtain, music plays softly*]

SCENE VII

The battlements of the mauve tower.
It is sunset and all the town is red.

13

The fountains seem to throw forth thousands of coloured jewels, for the water catches the colour of the sun.

As the scene progresses the palm trees turn from green to blue, from blue to violet, from violet to black. The sunflowers on the housetops bend their heads as if they weep. They look like rows of weeping women.

Upon the sea, a quantity of gorgeous-coloured sails pass along the horizon in the full glory of the setting sun.

To the left, upon the desert a long chain of camels walk so slowly that they seem to be standing still. They are wonderfully caparisoned in green and gold, and by their sides walk men dressed in long white robes; they wear upon their heads rose-coloured turbans embroidered with pearls.

Far away behind the town the moon rises slowly over the snow mountains.

The night is very calm, there is no sound to be heard.

Enter PRINCE LAON *and* PRINCESS INGRIA.

INGRIA: It is here where you spend all your days?

LAON: It is here.

[INGRIA *looks about her, she discovers a quantity of silks and fans lying upon the mosaic floor.*]

INGRIA: Oh! the beautiful green silks, the lovely white fans.

LAON: The sun is setting; see how all the town is burning red. [*He throws himself on to a golden carpet and with outstretched arms he watches the sky.*]

INGRIA: Why do you kneel to the sun?

LAON [*turning towards her with a strange smile*]: I . . . . . I kneel no longer to the sun, I kneel to you the moon.

INGRIA [*frightened*]: Oh! Oh! why do you talk to me like that?

LAON: How beautiful you are. May I not touch the crimson rubies in your hair? Your hair is like a pale red cloud, it is like a long chain of sweet red flowers. . . . What are the pale mauve stones that flash amidst your hair?

INGRIA: I do not know.

LAON: You do not know? [*A silence.*]

INGRIA: Oh see, see, the tower is reflected in the lake, I can see myself reflected in the lake. . . . I can see you too. . . . [*A silence.*] This morning when I saw your face reflected in the lake I was afraid.

LAON: Why, why were you afraid?

INGRIA: I do not know. [*A silence.*] Why did you pursue me with a sword?

LAON: I do not know.

INGRIA: We know nothing. [*A silence.*]

LAON [*suddenly*]: Oh! oh! I have left my sword in the garden, I have left my sword by the lake in the garden.

INGRIA [*dreamily*]: I can see it from here. Can you not see? There far below amidst the flowers at the foot of the tower. It looks like a serpent, it looks like a little yellow serpent.

LAON: I am afraid, let us go and seek it at once. They have never been able to take my sword away from me, I have never let them take my sword, and now I have left it by the lakeside in the garden.

INGRIA: Why should you be afraid? I am with you. [*A silence.*]

LAON: I do not know, but I feel that something terrible is going to happen. [*A silence.*]

INGRIA: See how beautiful the ships are upon the sea, they look like a cloud of birds with purple wings.

LAON: How red the sky is tonight. [*A pause.*] In the town I can hear drums. . . . [*They listen.*]

INGRIA [*softly*]: Yes, yes, someone is dead. [*A silence.*]

LAON [*looking intently at* INGRIA]: How pale you are Ingria, how pale you are. Your face is paler than silver, your mouth is redder than the sky, and your eyes look like two dying flowers.

INGRIA: You too are pale. [*A silence.*]

[*Suddenly on the staircase steps are heard, they sound at first far away but every moment grow louder.*]

LAON [*listening*]: Hush! What is that?

INGRIA: Perhaps it is Lieries, I told her to come to me at sunset on this tower.

LAON: Who is Lieries?

INGRIA: She is my slave.

[*The steps grow nearer, the scene is now almost dark. The moon has risen, but has not yet appeared above the tower, so that all the landscape*] is bathed in moonlight, but on the tower there is no light at all. Far away at sea there is a deep red line, which shows that the sun has not entirely disappeared. LAON *and* INGRIA *look like two shadows against the skyline. Then in the doorway three cloaked and hooded forms appear. They remain standing motionless without uttering a word.*]

INGRIA [*terrified*]: Oh! Oh! what is that? who are they?

LAON: My sword! My sword!

INGRIA: It is in the garden. Oh! Oh! I am afraid.

LAON [*whispering to* INGRIA]: They have come to kill me, they have come here to kill me. I will go to them. . . . They will not kill me at once, they will talk to me first, then while they are talking you will slip by me in the dark and warn the guards.

INGRIA: They are coming towards us. [*She clings to him.*] Oh, why do they not speak? I am afraid, I am afraid.

[*The three forms approach slowly.*]

LAON [*kissing her*]: Hush, hush, Ingria be brave, be brave.

INGRIA [*terrified*]: I can see their knives.

[*She pulls him with her towards the edge of the tower. Then slowly the three forms advance whilst* INGRIA *and* LAON *in each other's arms retreat backwards towards the parapet.*]

INGRIA [*suddenly*]: I have a dagger in my hair.

[LAON *puts his hand towards her hair and tries to find the dagger.*]

LAON [*faltering*]: Oh! Ingria I cannot find the dagger in your hair. Your hair is almost hid with precious stones. . . . I can no longer see. . . .

INGRIA [*fainting with fear and happiness*]: Kiss me! Kiss me. . . . [INGRIA *almost lifeless falls into* LAON's *arms.*]

LAON: I hear the wings of death about the tower.

[*All the time, in each other's arms, they retreat towards the parapet.*

Now LAON *has forgotten his sword, and is covering* INGRIA's *face with kisses.*

At last they reach the edge of the tower, which is bordered by a low wall.

They stand waiting. LAON *has his back to the three advancing figures, but* INGRIA *is watching them through half-closed eyes over* LAON's *shoulder.*

Then as she sees them lift their arms to strike, she utters a wild cry and seizing LAON *in her arms she almost lifts him on to the stone wall. There, for one last instant they stand together hovering against the sky like two shadows.*

Then as the three forms spring at them, LAON *and* INGRIA *jump together from the tower, and disappear into the night.*

There is a great silence.

Suddenly all the stars in the sky fall about the tower and the moon rising slowly falls upon the three black forms crouching over the parapet. Then far away a voice is heard singing, it grows nearer and nearer, and then in a full ray of moonlight LIERIES *appears upon the mauve tower. She is singing a strange melody accompanying herself with her harp. She looks about her seeking her mistress, then seeing three dim forms peering over the parapet she runs forward. The three shadows start up with a low cry. And the moon shines with a weird pale light upon three long grey knives.*

LIERIES *screams, rushes to the parapet and peers over. Far below she sees her mistress and* LAON *stretched out amongst the flowers at the foot of the mauve tower. Then crying and wringing her hands, she mounts on the stone wall, runs the complete length of the tower, wailing and calling her mistress by her name: "Ingria, Ingria . . . . . Ingria . . . . ." She looks round, sees the three black forms and the long grey knives, then with a cry of terror she flings herself from the tower and disappears.*

There is a long silence.

Then in the garden below a nightingale begins to sing, then another, and soon the whole garden becomes a world of song.

At the edge of the mauve tower crouch the three black forms peering over into the darkness; then suddenly they begin to laugh, to laugh, to laugh.

The birds cease singing and all the still night is made horrible with their laughter.

About the tower fall thousands of stars and far away in the east the first flush of the sun proclaims the beginning of another day.]

A DISCIPLE FROM THE COUNTRY

COMEDY IN AN ACT

CHARACTERS IN THE PLAY
(Duly labelled and thoroughly explained)

MRS CREAMWAY, *a wealthy Australian widow*
STELLA, *her daughter, known in Society as Saint Angelica*
LADY SEAFAIRER, *a paid chaperone*
MRS BLOSSOME, *an uneducated person who still believes in miracles*
LORD BLUEHARNIS, *in love with Stella*
MASON, *butler to Mrs Creamway*
FLORA, *a housemaid suffering from a polluted mind*

THE SCENE *is laid in Mrs Creamway's house in Mayfair*

SCENE: *The Saint's Boudoir. The room suggests a comfortable Oratory. On the walls religious reproductions of early Flemish Masters, Statuettes of Saints and Martyrs arranged in sociable little groups and sets on the mantelpiece, a large China bird, possibly a woodpecker, in their midst, strikes a personal note all its own. A Bishop's mitre, an embroidered cope, slung over a Louis Quinze screen, make a picturesque background for a luxurious-looking sofa, Religious books, musty with age—not use—piled up on small French tables. Profusions of flowers everywhere. A Tapestry curtain, centre, divides off a French drawing room, from whence comes the sound of a piano—Chopin's Prelude in A flat—may be distinguished, faintly. There is an air of unconvincing devotion about everything. The pink silk cushions on the sofa would never be tolerated by a canonized Saint, nor would the electric light-fittings, also of pink silk. As the* CURTAIN *rises, discover* STELLA *seated in a high-backed ecclesiastical-looking chair. A reading-table before her supports an immense folio; evidently a book on the Higher Life.* SHE *looks bored, reads a few moments, then picks up a mirror and examines her face attentively.* SHE *is about twenty-two, extremely pretty, beautifully dressed.*

A door bangs, SHE *hastily puts down the mirror, turning it round the glass-side from her, and resumes her book.*

A pause.

Enter MASON *the butler, an extremely pious-looking man who announces* "Lady Seafairer."

STELLA *does not look up,* SHE *appears absorbed in what she is reading.* LADY SEAFAIRER *is a woman of five and forty, stout, and rather worldly-looking, her gown at every movement betrays its French origin.*

21

LADY SEAFAIRER: My dear Stella, how lovely you look. I never know what you are wearing, stand up and let me see.

STELLA [*rising*]: I am white tonight, we are dining with Aunt Thedosia in Charles Street, I speak afterwards on "Purity" at Mrs Wembley's. See my Lilies how beautiful they are. They were a present from Lord Blueharnis.

LADY SEAFAIRER: A charming personality, but not the sort of man to accept Lilies from. And now tell me. Don't you think your hair is done just a trifle too high for a Saint?

STELLA: Mother would have me do it this way. She says from the end of a room one might mistake it for a Halo.

[*The piano in the adjoining room ceases.*]

LADY SEAFAIRER: You are certainly the most un-ordinary girl I have ever chaperoned. Do you know, Stella, I am becoming quite fond of your mother. She is so tactful, so full of resource, it is pleasant to think of all the amiable wealthy women that come from our colonies. [*Enter* MRS CREAMWAY.] Ah! here you are, dear Mrs Creamway, we were talking of you.

[MRS CREAMWAY *is a woman of ample figure, magnificently over-dressed.*]

MRS CREAMWAY: It is very reckless to talk about people in my house, where there are all curtains and no doors.

LADY SEAFAIRER: I was just telling Stella—or Angelica, as we must call her now—what a wise, sensible mother she has got.

MRS CREAMWAY [*beaming*]: Dear child! it makes me happy to think what a success she has become.

LADY SEAFAIRER: And quickly too. The last girl I chaperoned—a Miss Gossford—took me four summers, and a winter in Cairo. Happily she is married to one of Lord Cotswold's boys now. She was one of those difficult silent girls, it made me uneasy to sit in the same room with her. One morning she came in from riding in the sun and fainted. I never saw her look prettier; fainting suited her. "Do it again," I said, "do it again," and she did it most beautifully. That evening at the Opera we had stalls, just under the State Box. I always maintain that stalls are more advantageous for an unmarried girl. In a Box you may come and go unnoticed without disturbing a soul, but in the Stalls it is different. Well! just as Wotan was beginning to get the least bit wearisome Miss Gossford *swooned*. I was totally unprepared. Music seems to sap all the strength out of me. I just turned and looked at her. She was leaning to the left on the arm of a most distinguished-looking personage, looking, I am bound to say, perfectly charming. At that moment a slight tap on the right shoulder brought me to my senses. I looked up . . . I shivered . . . The Queen was handing me a glass of Brandy and water!

STELLA: And did Miss Gossford marry the distinguished-looking personage?

LADY SEAFAIRER [*mysteriously*]: He was the father. It was Lord Cotswold.

MRS CREAMWAY: Remember, Lady Seafairer, I want to see my child make a still more brilliant match than Miss Gossford's. I am prepared to sacrifice a great deal for Stella.

LADY SEAFAIRER: And she shall, she certainly shall, without a sacrifice of any kind, I hope. People already talk of her as Saint Angelica, it will be her own fault if she doesn't marry *at least* a Bishop. [*Confidentially:*] There are no fewer than fourteen single Bishops in England at this present moment, Mrs Creamway. Thirteen of them are widowers. Stella is artistic, in a Cathedral she would find scope for her tastes. Erecting a window to herself here, altering the position of a pulpit there, resting in the Sanctuary when she felt tired, making Daisy-chains for the dear Bishop as the Calendar decrees.

MRS CREAMWAY: You recall a little Australian sister-in-law of mine, who owns considerable property in the Bush. She has a mania for sketching Tombstones. She can draw best before Breakfast she used to say.

STELLA: I believe you are in love with a Bishop yourself Lady Seafairer!

LADY SEAFAIRER [*poetically*]: I am in love with a certain Cathedral that I know.

STELLA: It is sad that one may not be mistress of a Cathedral without belonging to a Bishop, and probably a whole Diocese besides! I could never marry a Bishop.

LADY SEAFAIRER [*shocked*]: Tut child! And you a Saint!

STELLA: Lady Seafairer, I became a Saint because I had tried being everything else. I was like so many other girls. I played golf a little, sang a little, did watercolour drawings—rural scenes—you know the kind of thing—cottages, with the smoke coming out at every chimney. I was horribly mediocre. I was ambitious and I longed for success. It was whilst we were in Florence that everything changed. Stopping at the same hotel as we were, there was an artist. A Mediævalist, I think he called himself. One day he stopped me on the stairs, and told me I reminded him of Saint Cecilia! He said that it was a thousand pities to see me in a serge walking-dress, when my type demanded something infinitely more flowing . . . more *Renaissance*. I was tremendously astonished as you can suppose, but not much offended, I thought the man just eccentric.

MRS CREAMWAY: Providentially I happened to pass by in the lift at that moment—laden with curios—my morning's shopping. I had with me some Venetian lace I remember, and a Papal throne. Imagine my feelings when I caught sight of Stella re-arranging her hair, on the public staircase, with the aid of a man, who had never even been introduced. "Insanity" I thought, and stopped the lift. To my surprise and indignation Stella asked the man up to our sitting room, and there, for nearly three hours, she allowed him to take, what seemed to my old-fashioned notions, nothing less than liberties with her person.

STELLA: All the while he was arranging me he talked of the magic of Suggestion. Some people should suggest the Sea he said, others look as though they lived curious lives, far away, out of the world, in some enchanted forest of their own; there were temperaments that could create atmosphere. Poor little Mrs Cavanah, who sat about half the day in draughts and places waiting for her husband, was, he said, most emphatically a Shepherdess. She suggested sheep. She was delighted when I informed her, and goes to Berger now for all her hats. "Think of the numbers and numbers of people who suggest nothing whatever, my dear," she said to me when I told her, "and besides it is nice to look as though one owned sheep, people will think I have a place in the country." I, on the other hand, recalled a victim of the Inquisition. There is a picture of me in Florence painted three hundred years ago as Saint Cecilia . . . Exactly me, except for a mole.

MRS CREAMWAY: The outrageous creature also had the audacity to tell me, that judging from my style of dress, I might have found things in common with Herodias.

LADY SEAFAIRER: That was very rude of him, and what did you say?

MRS CREAMWAY: My dear, what *could* I say but "Oh!"

LADY SEAFAIRER: I am glad you have told me all this: when I consented to chaperone your daughter, I was under the impression she had always been a Saint—a colonial one to be sure.

MRS CREAMWAY [*with pride*]: Who would suspect to see Stella now, she had passed her teens in the Bush?

LADY SEAFAIRER: I consider Stella's improvement very satisfactory. It must be gratifying for you, Mrs Creamway, to find yourself the mother of such a sweet, pliant girl, as a rule, religious people give me neuralgia, or rob me of my circulation, but with Stella it is otherwise. Like most of the world's attractive saints, she has a sympathetic knowledge of life's little foibles, and unlike them, she always manages to be perfectly dressed. I predict for her a radiant future, at all events in *this* world.

MRS CREAMWAY [*anxiously*]: I hope you don't foresee anything unpleasant for Stella in the next?

[*Enter* MASON, *followed a moment afterwards by* LORD BLUEHARNIS.]

MASON: Lord Blueharnis.

[LORD BLUEHARNIS *is a young man of five and twenty, good-looking, his Tailor beyond reproach.* HE *wears an eyeglass.*]

MRS CREAMWAY: Ah. Good evening, Lord Blueharnis, this is a delightful surprise.

LORD BLUEHARNIS: I came to know if it is true that the Saint is speaking on "Purity" tonight at Mrs Wembley's. I only heard this moment at the Club.

STELLA: Of course; but your Lilies? I thought you knew.

LORD BLUEHARNIS: Not a word. A lucky accident, I assure you.

STELLA: It was nice of you to send them me without any *arrière pensée.* Thanks.

LADY SEAFAIRER: I hope, Lord Blueharnis, you will not be too extravagant at your florist's this week, or you will have nothing left to spend at the Bazaar next Thursday. I am selling at your mother's stall. We have some very tempting-looking shells; a wonderful pink variety that let you hear the sea when you press them to your ears, and when these are all sold, as they probably will be, after a very few minutes, we have a provision of mysterious-looking Bulbs. Unfortunately your mother has mixed the tickets, so we shall scarcely know what we are selling.

LORD BLUEHARNIS: It's consoling to think that your mistakes will not be immediately found out.

LADY SEAFAIRER [*looking at her wrist*]: I had no idea it was so late. I am no longer as robust as I was, and have doctor's orders to lie down and rest before dressing for dinner. I shall read Stella's new book *The Red Rose of Martyrdom,* whilst my maid manicures me. Stella always binds her books in such ravishing colours. It is a pleasure to leave them lying about. [*Sighs deeply.*] Ah! What a clever, stately girl you have, Mrs Creamway. Take care of her! [*To* STELLA *as she passes out:*] We shall meet again this evening if my strength permits.

MRS CREAMWAY: I will see you to your carriage, Lady Seafairer.

[*Exit* MRS CREAMWAY *and* LADY SEAFAIRER.]

LADY SEAFAIRER [*voice outside*]: No, no, Mrs Creamway, I beg.

MRS CREAMWAY: Yes! Yes! Yes!

LADY SEAFAIRER [*voice faintly*]: It's a job Motor, the horses have caught cold.

LORD BLUEHARNIS: Saint! Stella! Why were you so cruel at Kempton Park last week, you never looked at me!

STELLA: Didn't I? I was frightfully busy trying to kill two birds with the same stone. You know that I am to speak at Manchester House on the "Curse of Racing" before the Season is over? Well, my time was too occupied with hanging on the carmine lips of Mrs Waterport who knew a good thing, and gathering notes for my lecture to be able to bow to all my friends. [*Joyfully:*] I have bought some beautiful Malines lace with my winnings.

LORD BLUEHARNIS: You know, Stella, I always think that in spite of your curious style of dress, you are the most modish woman in London. I shall never forget the first time I saw you. You were wearing violet silk and emeralds, I was enslaved!

STELLA: Firstly, my gown was *not* silk, it was crêpe de chine; secondly, you have no right to speak to me like this dearest George—you are not free to do so.

26

LORD BLUEHARNIS: Don't be prudish, Stella. You mean Dolly Witney, I suppose? Hers is a birdlike nature, she only hops where there are crumbs.

STELLA: And you have thrown enough to make a loaf. She has a sheaf of your letters, she told me so.

LORD BLUEHARNIS: Rhadamanthus!

STELLA: What do you say?

LORD BLUEHARNIS: Rhadamanthus. It is either Egyptian or Syrian for Cat! I forget which. But Stella, if I can settle things with Dolly, will you say I have a slight chance?

STELLA: If you wish me to say so, there might be a very, very slight one.

[*Re-enter* MRS CREAMWAY.]

MRS CREAMWAY: My child, I wonder whether you could perform a miracle for me. Quite a small one. There is a bone in my bodice piercing into my flesh, and Estelle has gone to the theatre.

[LORD BLUEHARNIS *turns away modestly, and picks up books on table, reads their titles,* The Pursuit of Perfection, Thomas à Kempis, Saint Thomas Aquinas.]

MRS CREAMWAY: Thanks dear, now I can breathe. [*To* LORD BLUEHARNIS:] I see you are interested in Stella's library, Lord Blueharnis, dear child, she has a passion for books that one cannot obtain everywhere. Only yesterday I spent most of my morning hunting for a pamphlet which satisfactorily proves that Mary Magdalen was actually engaged to John the Baptist. It was only after the sad affair at the Palace that Mary really buckled to, and became what she afterwards became. They tell me the whole thing has been turned quite recently into a very tuneful opera. In these days nobody seems safe from being set to music. My chief dread is that Stella will one day sicken of the world and leave me for a convent.

STELLA: Dear mother, believe me that I shall think twice before taking such a step.

MRS CREAMWAY: You could never stand the early hours, love, up at four —and I believe no breakfast to speak of. It is all very well in a proper climate amidst flowers and sunshine, but in England it is wiser not to trifle with one's health. To be well and unailing is a gift from Heaven, and I am convinced that our Maker does not wish us to be careless of ourselves. Quite the contrary!

LORD BLUEHARNIS: You have very comforting views of life, Mrs Creamway, and I agree with you.

MRS CREAMWAY [*irrelevantly, but with meaning*]: How I wish that I had had a son!

LORD BLUEHARNIS [*densely*]: I wonder whose house you would have sent him to at Eton.

MRS CREAMWAY: I don't suppose that I should have ever been able to part with him, the darling boy!

STELLA: Don't talk about him, mother, or I shall think that you regret having me!

MRS CREAMWAY: My own Stella, how could that be possible!

LORD BLUEHARNIS: What a wonderful photograph of your daughter in this week's *Peacock,* Mrs Creamway. Quite remarkable.

STELLA: Oh! I have not seen it. Does it put who I am?

LORD BLUEHARNIS: Yes. It says, "Saint Angelica—The beautiful heiress, Miss Creamway," and follows it up with a little biography of your mother.

MRS CREAMWAY [*nervously*]: That was very thoughtful of the Editor. I can only hope that it is correct. The very word *biography* makes me shiver. When I remember the biography they wrote of Mr Creamway in the *Melbourne Post,* I turn quite faint at the word.

STELLA: But my picture in the *Peacock!* You would have laughed if you could have seen the photographer striking the match for the flames. I thought the Studio would have caught on fire.

LORD BLUEHARNIS: It certainly looked a warm way to be photographed, though your expression, Miss Creamway . . . It seemed to me that no one could look like that without feeling inspired in some way or another.

STELLA: The photographer just said, look out of that window, and do not start when I light the fuse. I remember I counted the sparrows on the rooftops over the way, until I felt that if I went on counting them any more, I should end in looking like one.

MRS CREAMWAY [*puzzled*]: Stella is so fugitive. How should she look like a sparrow by merely counting them? One might just as well take the appearance of a sheep after sleeplessness, although as a rule I am generally picturing the Shepherd as I pass through the gate. And now my child, we must really be starting for your aunt's.

STELLA: Wait for me a few moments, Mamma, whilst I tidy my Halo.

[*Exit* STELLA.]

MRS CREAMWAY: I am afraid as a rule you find Saints more austere, Lord Blueharnis?

LORD BLUEHARNIS: I am not in the habit of meeting them often, Mrs Creamway, but your daughter seems to me to be perfection.

MRS CREAMWAY: That is very nice of you to say so. [*Seats herself comfortably on sofa.*] Will you kindly hand me that Ilex-wood box. Thank you. I know so well Stella's "few moments," and I am growing weary of these socks—I often wonder whether I should have the patience to do a pair of combinations, alas! I fear not. [*She takes out a pale blue sock and begins to knit.*]

LORD BLUEHARNIS: It must be deadly, knitting a big affair in white.

MRS CREAMWAY: Oh! I never restrict myself to colours; as a rule I work easiest in heliotrope—but to go back to Stella, I will not dissemble from you, Lord Blueharnis, that my child in home life hides a beautiful nature, under what might seem to be imprudent flippancy. She is in many ways a mystic—I have it from her maid, who should certainly know. And what is more, I am afraid she too constantly exhausts herself needlessly, and wearies Heaven by long and arduous prayers for all our welfares. Only the other day at the Opera, Mrs Goring said to me: "Your girl has a frail, intellectual expression, and I should say would not live long." I cannot help worrying a great deal about Stella.

LORD BLUEHARNIS: I am surprised to hear it, I had always thought of your daughter as exceptionally hardy.

MRS CREAMWAY: Hardy! What a dreadful expression. I would sooner see Stella indisposed than hardy. Hardy girls are generally forward, and invariably sly. In my opinion the child is relaxed, run down. When a girl is fond of Gregorian music there is generally something wrong.

LORD BLUEHARNIS: With such a matchless complexion as Stella's, there cannot be anything very serious.

29

MRS CREAMWAY: We are going to recuperate the ravages of a London season in an Italian garden.

LORD BLUEHARNIS: How beautiful it sounds. Do you mean actually in Italy or somewhere on the Thames?

MRS CREAMWAY [*dreamily*]: The Thames, the Upper Thames.

LORD BLUEHARNIS: May I be allowed to come and visit you when you are in Italy?

MRS CREAMWAY: We shall be delighted. Our station is St Catherine-in-the-Marsh, half an hour from Paddington—you must change at Ripley Junction.

LORD BLUEHARNIS: I shall remember.

MRS CREAMWAY: The house is said to be haunted, but since I have put in electric light nobody has seen anything to speak of. Stella's presence, no doubt, has had a soothing influence over the restless spirit. The intrepid girl has sat up alone more than once, with her Kodak and a bunch of keys.

LORD BLUEHARNIS: Why keys?

MRS CREAMWAY: For fear the ghost might have left compromising letters in one of the cupboards and wished to destroy them.

[*Enter* STELLA.]

STELLA: I am quite ready.

MRS CREAMWAY [*timidly, criticising her daughter's attire*]: Stella, love, I don't think you should carry a fan—a fan is scarcely synonymous with Purity, and a Saint cannot be too careful of small matters in a censorious world. Saint Teresa I am sure would be horrified if she could see you. I approve of the Lilies, but *not* the fan.

STELLA: Lord Blueharnis, I appeal to you.

LORD BLUEHARNIS: Unquestionably I think a Saint should carry a fan, if only to hide her blushes from a coarse world.

STELLA: Then that settles it.

LORD BLUEHARNIS [*shaking hands with* MRS CREAMWAY]: Au revoir, Mrs Creamway, we shall meet again at the lecture I hope. I am sure it will be a novel experience for our hostess; it is not often one can gather Lilies at Number 39!

MRS CREAMWAY [*pensively*]: I am surprised. Mrs Wembley has always struck me as being the very picture of health and inexperience. You have been misinformed I think, for I have remarked more than once her wonderful Arum Lilies. [*To* STELLA:] My child how quick you have been, usually your few moments run into three quarters of an hour, I will not keep you five minutes, I am so anxious to try and get the toe finished to this blue sock. The blue is a little vivid, but with a darker shade of garters . . . [*To* MASON *who enters:*] Yes Mason what is it?

MASON: If you please, Madam, there is an old woman downstairs who asks to see Miss Stella.

STELLA: Who can it be? Is she quite respectable?

MASON [*in discreet voice*]: I should say not Miss. She had no visiting cards—forgot them in her Sunday skirt, she informed me; gives her name as Jane Blossome, owns a piggery in Warwickshire. She has walked all the way to London to see you Miss.

MRS CREAMWAY: A piggery! What is a piggery?

MASON [*respectfully*]: A residence for pigs, Madam.

MRS CREAMWAY [*alarmed to* STELLA]: My child take care! This person may have designs upon you. No really nice woman would walk all the way from Warwickshire; besides the very length of her walk would make her unpleasant—I mistrust her intentions. Mason you had better send her away. I have my suspicions that we may have destroyed something belonging to her whilst motoring.

STELLA: Oh! mother, you don't think the dreadful cries we heard last Sunday on the Stratford road could have come from Mr Blossome?

MRS CREAMWAY: Nonsense! those were Mrs Maberley's Peacocks, warning me not to wear my Pompadour costume at the Christhorps' garden party, as it was going to rain.

MASON: She does not appear to be bent on mischief Miss, an old hobbledehoy out for an airing, I should say. There is nothing malignant about her appearance.

STELLA: Very well then Mason, show her up.

[*Exit* MASON.]

LORD BLUEHARNIS: Perhaps you would sooner I didn't stay?

31

MRS CREAMWAY: No don't leave us, we may want your protection. [*Apologetically:*] I am afraid I have no weapons. Those mediæval hatchets on the staircase are so high up, one can only reach them with a ladder.

STELLA: My dear mother, how ridiculous you are! Do you suppose the woman is carrying a loaded revolver!

MRS CREAMWAY [*upset*]: I am sure my child I don't know.

[*Enter* MRS BLOSSOME. *She is a charming old lady, draped from head to heels in a many-coloured shawl. In her right hand she holds a long stave to which is fastened a gorgeous handkerchief, bulky with provisions—in her left hand a superb bouquet of wildflowers. At the sight of* MRS CREAMWAY *she falls on her knees, her flowers extended in offering, murmuring in raptures:* "Saint! Saint!"]

MRS CREAMWAY [*taken back*]: There is some trifling mistake. Address your petitions to this young lady. I am only her mother!

STELLA [*kindly*]: What do you want me to do?

MRS BLOSSOME [*in ecstasies*]: Oh! the sweet young lamb, at last I sees you! [*Stroking the hem of* STELLA's *frock:*] Oh! the clean white robe! Washed by the angels, I can see. No laundry ever scrubbed them frillies— done in Heaven to the sound of harps.

STELLA: How clever of you to have guessed. A little French Nun made me this. She is starting a Millinery establishment of her own in the Avenue Malakoff.

MRS CREAMWAY [*enlighteningly*]: Just off the Elysian Fields. I daren't say it in French.

MRS BLOSSOME: The Elysian Fields! Where the saints sit all day on garden seats and warm their hands in the sun?

MRS CREAMWAY [*contentedly wrapped in her own thoughts*]: Quite close. In front of one of those Embassies, I have forgotten which, the third floor, but fortunately there's a lift. You cannot mistake the place, besides, "Aux Anges élégants" is written in Gothic characters across the door.

STELLA: There is generally a violin going and some tea. Then, afterwards, when the incense that is always kept burning before the prettiest gowns has gone a little to one's head and one is feeling thoroughly amiable and extravagant, Mademoiselle Gabrielle appears and tempts one with a fur wrap or a Renaissance fan.

MRS BLOSSOME: The wicked hussy! but we need only open the Bible to see how Saints was always sorely tried.

LORD BLUEHARNIS: You delicious old woman! Aren't you a portrait by Raeburn or Reynolds come to life, and wandering away from your frame? There is a picture of you selling apples somewhere; I think it's in Trafalgar Square. There will be a big reward for you in the morning. Will you come and stay at my house until then? We are very hard up, and have never yet had a reward.

MRS BLOSSOME: Reward indeed! Apple woman indeed! I am no zany, young man! And let me tell you that I keep pigs, and thems worth more than apples. My husband, poor man, was an artist, he used to carve fancy objects out of acorns until . . .

MRS CREAMWAY [*with a cry*]: Until! Then those were your husband's last words! I had hoped they were Mrs Maberley's Peacocks. [*She collapses.*]

MRS BLOSSOME [*tranquilly*]: Until he was made the Sexton at Queen's Cray Church, that turned his head. He died designing his own grave. His last words were he didn't wish to be disturbed. "Choose your own resting-place Jane," he said, "and don't fret me." Oh! I was glad the neighbours weren't there to hear! If only to avoid gossip I must go against his last will, the Lord forgive me.

STELLA: A most disturbing case of heartlessness. I am surprised that an Englishman should hold such opinions. Even the Egyptians insisted on not being separated at the last. I recollect the final act of *Aïda,* the unhappy wife perishing alive in her husband's tomb, as the curtain slowly and painfully falls. I do not know which extreme is the most to be condemned.

MRS CREAMWAY: If this is the sad business that brings you to London, I am afraid we can do little for you. I have no influence with cemetery officials. Let me lend you a little book, a *Life of Saint John Chrysostom,* it is the most helpful thing I can think of just now.

MRS BLOSSOME: Thank you Mam, we have a Carnegie Liberary in our village, and it's done nobody benefit yet, except to maintain Tabatha Tyrwhit in idleness; it's she that's supposed to range the great folk's lives, and keep the female books apart from the males, respectable-like, and God forgive her if she don't. It's Tabatha that's supposed to dust the map of the world, that you can see drooping through the window from the road, and never does she trouble to lift her arm higher than Scotland. Many's the time I've sat in the parlour of the Cap and Bells, over the way, and tried to pick out the Holy Land at a distance, and it's then that I've seen Tabatha Tyrwhit scarcely so much as flick at her own country with her duster. No, Lady, it's not for no borrowing of books I come to you about, for they disgusts me! I've called here this afternoon to be permanently cured.

MRS CREAMWAY [*much surprised*]: Permanently cured?

MRS BLOSSOME: You see Mam, I suffer cruel from aches and pains; comes from tending pigs on the heath. Last winter I spent in hospital—a fatiguing place. I fair pined to go back to me pigs. It was in hospital I first heard tell of your Sainted daughter, Lady. One afternoon the parson's wife brings me picture papers. "Liven the monotony Jane," she says, "and me husband will come and pray over you when he's a few minutes to hisself, to cheer you up," she says, and she departs leaving me the papers. No sooner had the lady gone than I relaxes out of me tortured position, seeing as there was no jelly or grapes to be had that day, and begins turning over her illustrations. In each of them there Weeklies I sees the same sweet face. "Saint Angelica," it says, "Martyr," it says, and shews the poor young lamb being burnt to death with faggots. "Shame!" I exclaims, "to harm so gentle a thing," and questions the nurse in charge concerning the matter. "Saints is extinct," she says scornful-like and takes the illustrations away, and gives them to Mrs Ballie to make up for an Elm tree falling down on her prize Hollyhocks. "Mrs Blossome is delirious," I hears her tell the doctor, "Leave her quiet," he answers, and I lies there and thinks. "Quick Jane," I tells my-self, "the Saint may be only scorched, go to her, and she will cure you for the love of Heaven."

STELLA: And, you see, I am not even singed!

MRS BLOSSOME: Your poor feet! Who can say how they are, hid away under that Elysian robe.

MRS CREAMWAY: Poor old woman! Couldn't we rub her with something? I don't like to think she has had her long walk for nothing. She is probably only rheumatic, a little of that extract of mine, and a glass of old Port might work wonders. Phipps shall take her back to Warwickshire in the motor, she will enjoy the ride.

LORD BLUEHARNIS: How indulgent you always are Mrs Creamway! I believe you have hit the very thing.

MRS CREAMWAY: Stella, love, get the extract from my medicine chest—it's a tall threatening-looking bottle, labeled poison—you cannot mistake it; be careful not to upset any, as the stain never comes out.

[*Exit* STELLA.]

MRS BLOSSOME: Has the young lamb gone to fetch the miracles?

MRS CREAMWAY: Yes, and in a very few minutes, I hope, you will feel soothed. Close your eyes, and rest until she comes and try to feel grateful to Heaven, that through our efforts you may perhaps be cured.

MRS BLOSSOME: Only perhaps? Then have I worn out the soles of my boots for nothing?

MRS CREAMWAY: There! There! don't fret. [*Conversationally:*] I am sure the country is looking very pretty just now—those lovely ferns and foxgloves are a great treat to us. Such flowers unfortunately are unobtainable at a London florist's.

MRS BLOSSOME [*becoming chatty*]: They comes from the garden of an old body who styles herself the Countess Hoop!

MRS CREAMWAY: Really! how very interesting, I know her quite well!

MRS BLOSSOME: I never see anyone so roused! If it had been the Church bells, or the stable clock that had been took, she couldn't have said more.

[*Enter* STELLA *with a decanter of Port wine and a medicine bottle.*]

STELLA: Here are things that are going to do you good! Drink the wine first, and then tell us where you feel the aches most.

MRS BLOSSOME [*uncomplainingly*]: Back and front, Miss, is the worst.

MRS CREAMWAY: A good Massage is what she wants and climate! A pity she is not more accomplished or I would send her straight out to Switzerland as companion to old Lady Hannah Gore. I know she is wanting one. The last woman I recommended her turned out so unsatisfactory that Lady Hannah pushed her over a crevasse. The creature used positively to *hiss* at Lady Hannah at the smallest provocation. Her end was richly deserved. I should so like to make the dowager amends by finding her a real treasure this time, but you see I know so little of Mrs Blossome that I hardly like to take the risk, and a second death at my door would be too injurious to my health now that summer is so nearly over. Dr Mannering was scolding me only yesterday at not taking more care of myself. I very nearly promised him to do no more entertaining until the new year. Society is terribly relaxing, and I think that Stella and I should disappear. But I am wandering from the point! What are we going to do with Mrs Blossome.

MRS BLOSSOME [*who has finished her Port, dreamily*]: I feel deliciously tired, only me hands ache now.

LORD BLUEHARNIS: Let's rub them for her.

[THEY *kneel round* MRS BLOSSOME *and begin rubbing her.* MRS CREAM-WAY *after a moment starts beating the air with a Louis XV fan, at the same time holding a scent-bottle to* MRS BLOSSOME'*s nostrils.*]

MRS BLOSSOME [*soothed*]: I feels as though I was driving along in a carriage of my own, the trees a-shady and the Saints a-singing carols in the fields.

MRS CREAMWAY: Poor old lady, she is wandering. What a picturesque mind! I hope she doesn't mean to die here, that would be too awkward. Stella, my child, I think you had better see Phipps about the motor immediately.

MRS BLOSSOME [*enjoying herself*]: No, young lady, don't take your cool hand away. When I feel the vibration of saintliness so near the pain grows less.

LORD BLUEHARNIS: Your magic touch, Stella!

MRS CREAMWAY: I believe she made up her mind to be cured before she came, sensible woman. She should find her career in Christian Science. [*Vaguely:*] A few lessons in elocution and she would sway crowds.

MRS BLOSSOME: A little more of that Porty-wine, and then I must be moving if I wants to see any of the sights. It's been a consolation to have rested me limbs in these Cathedral surroundings [*glancing at the pictures and statuettes*], and now that I feels restored and myself again by the soft touch of your flutey fingers, Miss, I must be a-going. My pains are gone thank the Lord—I feels towards you all warmth of heart and giddiness of mind now that I know that Saints is not extinct.

STELLA: Oh! Mother listen to her! Really I believe this is a case of miracle. What pleasure it would give me to be interviewed with her for one of the Church Magazines.

MRS CREAMWAY: What a happy idea, I will telephone for a reporter—but we must not confine ourselves quite exclusively to the Church Gazettes, unfortunately they are too seldom read by the right sort.

LORD BLUEHARNIS: As a Saint's mother, what do you consider the right sort, Mrs Creamway?

MRS CREAMWAY [*with great decision*]: A person with a permanent Opera Box, Lord Blueharnis, and a habitable fortress in the North.

LORD BLUEHARNIS: I am afraid with such ideals you could never look with indulgence on a simple cottage in Surrey.

MRS CREAMWAY: A great deal would depend upon the landlord. A well-born man is capable of redeeming his surroundings, be they where they may.

LORD BLUEHARNIS: I wish my little cottage could hear you say so. Unfortunately it has no idea of being redeemed, or it might find a means of closing its hospitality to rats.

MRS CREAMWAY [*in a tone of voice she would use to an invalid not expected to recover*]: Rats! my poor friend! . . . [*Then with forced cheerfulness:*] I can tell you of some wonderful traps that only require half the usual amount of cheese. And now, Stella, give Mrs Blossome another glass of Port, and I will telephone immediately for the interviewer to come post-haste. As you say, I think this cure is a phenomenon granted by Heaven, and should not miss to be chronicled. [*Kissing* STELLA *as she hurries out:*] Oh! my wonderful girl!

STELLA: Whilst mother is ringing up the exchange, let us arrange about our futures. All the while the miracle was working in Mrs Blossome I was thinking of you, George, perhaps that was why my hand was so soft and caressing.

LORD BLUEHARNIS: Stella dear, do you really care for me? Enough to marry me I mean?

STELLA: Of course, George! Exterminate those rats and we will spend our honeymoon in Surrey. I have always longed to live in the country, away from Mamma, and keep poultry. I should like to be celebrated for white Dorkings, which would be difficult whilst you allowed rats.

LORD BLUEHARNIS: You curious child! [*Kisses her.*]

MRS BLOSSOME [*coughing*]: Can you buy Porty-wine at the Chemist's, Miss?

STELLA [*startled*]: No, I don't think you can! Hush! Rest and thank Heaven for your recovery until the interviewer arrives; he will take down all your words so be very careful how you choose them! I think you should begin by giving a little sketch of your early life, and then say how it came about that mysterious voices guided you to our door.

[MRS CREAMWAY *re-enters almost in tears.*]

MRS CREAMWAY: It's too vexatious! There are no available reporters. Apparently there are first nights at all the theatres, and everybody seems to be having a dance. Stella, we are already too late for your aunt's dinner. I have telephoned to say I have had a sudden return of my old sickness caused by unavoidably sitting with my back to the horses. Unhappily the lecture remains, but there are still two hours before that. And now I will propose a little scheme—I suggest that, if Lord Blueharnis will help us, we should *write the interview ourselves.* Mrs Harry-Henry, the charming editoress of the *Smart World,* has promised to insert anything we may see fit.

LORD BLUEHARNIS: All my skill is at your service. This will not be the first time that I have played the part of interviewer. As a war correspondent I used constantly to gather the impressions of the captives.

STELLA: Then let us start at once. One tiny word before you begin! I want to tell you that my dress is a copy of a Botticelli in the National Gallery, and was made in Paris. Your feminine readers would not wish for silence on this matter. Perhaps a suitable opportunity has arrived for me to say that the black Tuscan straw hat I wore lately at Ascot, with the cascades of blue and pink Wisteria, came from Claude of the Rue de la Paix. Mr Waterbury, the owner of Sulky Max, said that his horse's miraculous win was due to me. Immediately the animal perceived my Wisteria nodding in the wind, it became perfectly possessed and *flew.* It was a most gratifying advertisement to Madame Claude, who immediately deducted off my account the cost of the trimmings. I think with absolute confidence you may predict to your readers that, for the racecourse in future, Wisteria will be the flower à la mode.

[SHE *goes over to the mirror, puffs out her hair, then seats herself comfortably in easy chair, her hands clasped, and waits for interviewer to begin.*]

MRS CREAMWAY [*hurriedly*]: One small word! You might say that her mother is a connection of old Admiral Van Boome, the terror of most Americans, and that a great-aunt of hers was famed for the costliness of her lace, and her unassailable reputation. These small hereditary matters may be of importance. Pray take a seat.

LORD BLUEHARNIS: I am afraid Mrs Blossome is no longer awake. [*A faint snore from* MRS BLOSSOME.] We must turn her out of that comfortable chair if we are to have any satisfactory results.

MRS CREAMWAY [*Shaking* MRS BLOSSOME. *Solemnly and with emphasis*]: Your hour has come Mrs Blossome. I hope you are prepared to truthfully answer all the questions this gentleman may see wise to put to you.

MRS BLOSSOME: Another glass of that Porty-wine before I answers any of your questions. [*A little huffy.*]

MRS CREAMWAY [*complying*]: This must be absolutely your last. And now come and sit on this nice Chippendale chair, and tell us in your own words the story of your life. I am going to efface myself utterly; but I shall not rest idle. I intend to make a little pencil portrait of you that shall be published with your narrative. You will enjoy having your likeness done, will you not? It is not often that one can be drawn for nothing!

[MRS BLOSSOME *sips her Port a moment in silence, uneasily watching* MRS CREAMWAY's *movements.* MRS CREAMWAY *provides herself with drawing utensils, and retires to background. From time to time during the following scene, she extends her pencil, screws up her eyes, and proceeds to take mysterious measurements of* MRS BLOSSOME's *body.*]

STELLA: Well! Mrs Blossome we are waiting for you to begin. Remember to be perfectly natural, and do not tie yourself too much to the truth if you can think of something better instead.

LORD BLUEHARNIS: I am listening.

MRS BLOSSOME [*finishes her Port, and begins her story with animation*]:

I was the beauty of our family. The bonniest lass you ever did see! Not a lad in the country round that didn't propose hisself in marriage, but I was one of them proud girls, and not easy to be pleased. It was after me twenty-fifth birthday that I says to myself: "It's time you settled down, Garth my dear"— that, Sir, was my maiden name—"and give up your carryings-on." Well! The day I accepted William Blossome there wasn't one that didn't say I might have done better for meself! "Throw yourself away, Jane," they says, but there! in them days I was in love.

LORD BLUEHARNIS: I think you might pass over your early married life, and begin narrating your experiences from the time of your widowhood. That should be enough.

MRS BLOSSOME [*shaking her head*]: Ah! that was a sad day, and one that William Blossome should blush to remember, be he where he may!

LORD BLUEHARNIS: It would not be an indiscretion to hint that your married life was not a success.

MRS BLOSSOME: Sir, I was deceived from the Altar.

LORD BLUEHARNIS [*to* STELLA]: This is the most sensational "interview" I can remember.

STELLA [*impatiently at first, gradually her voice becomes persuasive, lastly purely artificial*]: But the Voices! tell us about the Voices that guided you here. You were tending pigs, I think you said—almost like Joan of Arc —no doubt amidst extremely picturesque scenery. I know Warwickshire quite well. Then you must have noticed perhaps a reflection of me in the sky? or in a stream? or not unlikely a gentle voice murmured to you through the trees urging you to undertake a long and arduous journey, carrying only a staff, and a coloured handkerchief with your simple needs. Warning you, through some mystic Agency I cannot at this moment determine, to leave your swine, and thatched dwelling, in the hands of providence, and to seek on foot the aid of a beautiful maiden hidden in the twilight atmosphere of a London drawing room. Have I guessed right?

MRS BLOSSOME: Yes. I like to think of it happening just like that.

STELLA: And when you arrived in the West End, tired and footsore, no doubt the voices increased. [*Anxiously:*] Perhaps you heard harps?

MRS BLOSSOME: No Miss, I can't say that I did, but the voices does get louder, and the traffic do become thicker, so that if it hadn't been for a handsome and saucy-spoken policeman, I should have *never* durst cross the street.

STELLA: I thought so. The voices grew louder. [*To* LORD BLUEHARNIS:] Put it down, George; it is the most important evidence we have had yet.

LORD BLUEHARNIS: Give her a chance, Stella, you are doing all the work.

MRS BLOSSOME [*warming to her tale*]: And when at last I find the house with the aid of the newspaper cutting I has in my pocket, I pause, and asks myself which of the bells will I ring, "servants" or "visitors"—I see no bell marked "Disciples." "Visitors" I decides and pulls: counting seven for luck. Nobody comes. For the first time a feeling of Homesickness creeps over me, at the sight, maybe, of them shivery small trees in the centre of the square, with their sooty little sparrows. "Call yourself a *bird?*" I says to a sparrow, "if you was to show yourself in our part of the country, not even a Hawk would notice you." Then as still nobody comes to the door, I pulls again. This time the servants' bell. I waits and again counts seven—nothing appears. Seven times I counts seven, making forty-nine, a charmed number. That gives me an idea. I pulls both bells together with all my force. After that it was not long until someone came.

STELLA: I daresay there is some hidden meaning in all this. Your ringing once, and not being admitted. Your ringing twice, and still no answer. Your ringing a third time, a *double* ring, and this time your wonderful perseverance is rewarded with success. An Eastern would attach various symbolic meanings to the masterful way you grappled with the bell. Meanings which a Northern climate will not allow one to penetrate.

MRS CREAMWAY [*still busily sketching*]: Then I'm afraid you were kept waiting a few moments in the hall.

MRS BLOSSOME [*politely*]: Scarcely long enough to admire the statuary—young Scamps! but lads will be lads.

LORD BLUEHARNIS: Are you referring to the Ganymede, or to the Antinous?

MRS BLOSSOME [*with decision*]: Both Sir. Saucy to stand there like that, I says, before respectable visitors. If I could only reach up to you, my lads, I says, I'd give you a spanking.

MRS CREAMWAY [*plaintively*]: Pray do not excite yourself, Mrs Blossome, if you move now my drawing is forever spoilt!

STELLA: And then you were shown into my boudoir. Now tell me your exact impressions when you first saw me.

MRS BLOSSOME: Well Miss, I was all of a-tremble, me legs shook, and I fell on me knees at the sight of such extravagance.

STELLA [*to* LORD BLUEHARNIS]: "She was all of a-tremble." Have you got that down?

MRS CREAMWAY: I think you mistook me for my daughter?

MRS BLOSSOME: At first I was dazzled at the sight of your hair, Lady, gleaming with precious stones, but when I looks at you again, I says no! She's too stout for a Saint. Saints is always thin, and they bends towards you flexible-like as might a Bullrush.

STELLA: And then, when, with a joyful cry, you recognised me, I hope you heard far-off strains of music, and you knew that your sufferings were at a close.

MRS BLOSSOME: Yes, I hears the far-off strain of a Barbery-organ and I feels the waste of so many notes, and no one dancing! Then you strokes me, and gives me Porty-wine, and it feels as though I was caught up into the air and made a fuss of and then let gently down again, and me head is still a bit swimmy from being so new to having wings.

STELLA: You were probably sustained by happy spirits. And now rejoice that you are going back in a few moments to your country home, in the comfort of a new Mercèdes Automobile—you will find it fitted up with all the toilet requisitions you can dream of, but you have such a vivid complexion already that you scarcely need any rouge.

MRS CREAMWAY [*with an immense sigh, of work accomplished*]: Mrs Blossome, your portrait is finished, and I think that I can modestly say it is a masterpiece. I have draped you in a robe after my own inspiration and placed on your head one of those curious Welsh chimney hats that people so wrongly associate with witches. It is striking, is it not? [*Hands her portrait.*]

MRS BLOSSOME: Lord-a-mercy! is this me?

MRS CREAMWAY [*beaming*]: It is indeed.

STELLA [*looking at it*]: Oh, mother!

LORD BLUEHARNIS [*staring through his eyeglass*]: My dear Mrs Creamway.

MRS CREAMWAY [*explaining*]: I think the background is audacious. It is of course allegorical.

MRS BLOSSOME [*awed, her eyes glued to the sketch*]: And what are these?

MRS CREAMWAY [*smiling benevolently*]: Wings! I was in trouble with one of your arms, I think it was such a clever way out of the difficulty.

LORD BLUEHARNIS: Mrs Harry-Henry should sell the next number of the *Smart World* without the least difficulty.

STELLA: I am so glad we are going to be useful to her. She has always been so kind in writing pretty little half-truths about me, and has told me so much about myself I never knew before, that I cannot help feeling grateful to her. [*Taking* LORD BLUEHARNIS's *hand:*] George beloved, wouldn't this be a beautiful opportunity to announce our engagement?

MRS CREAMWAY: Your engagement? Stella! Oh, my child! [*Clasps her in her arms.*] I shall be unstrung all tomorrow. Lord Blueharnis you do not know the treasure you are taking from me; the crutch on whom, for many years, I have so tenderly leaned, but I see plainly that remonstrance would be useless, nay—selfish!

LORD BLUEHARNIS: I hope, Mrs Creamway, you will give your consent.

MRS CREAMWAY: On one condition, that the marriage shall take place immediately. I have always disliked long engagements. Anything like suspense is more than my nervous system can bear.

STELLA: I shall start my trousseau tomorrow. I am afraid this will mean a fortnight in Paris. My husband-to-be, can you endure this long parting?

LORD BLUEHARNIS: My sweetest! and after that we will live happily ever afterwards.

MRS CREAMWAY: I never heard two people so sanguine about the future before.

MRS BLOSSOME: To think that the *Voices* should end in *wedding bells*. It's at the Cannon's mouth I leaves you standing, Miss, but where's the use of argument when a maid's in love.

[*Enter* MASON.]

MASON: The Car is at the door, Madam. [*To* MRS BLOSSOME:] Have you your own motor goggles or will you borrow a visitor's pair?

MRS BLOSSOME: Thank you, I will borrow willingly. [*To* MRS CREAMWAY:] Perhaps I may be allowed to keep them to use afterwards as spectacles, as me eyes is not what they used.

MRS CREAMWAY: Certainly, but I am afraid they will not magnify as much as you could wish, I have told Mason to put in with you a few bottles of Port and some sandwiches so that you will not starve on the road.

MRS BLOSSOME: That Porty-wine is worth all me sufferings.

[MASON *hands her a pair of motor glasses which she puts on.*]

MRS CREAMWAY: Good-bye, Mrs Blossome, it has all been very pleasant— Stella's miracle I mean—clever girl! I shall so enjoy reading about it in tomorrow's paper. We shall probably be besieged with callers these next few days, I am afraid it will oblige me to arrange fresh flowers in the morning, although it isn't my day.

LORD BLUEHARNIS: One moment Mrs Blossome, will you kindly leave your address in the hall. As a contributor, you are entitled to a free copy of the *Smart World*. You will find all about yourself under the heading of "A Miracle in Mayfair." Good-bye, it has been such a pleasure meeting you.

STELLA: Before you go I want to be allowed to kiss you. Remember I am your patron saint now—wait I will give you a little relic of mine—this handkerchief, it may act as a charm.

MRS BLOSSOME [*pressing it to her lips*]: Violets! Ah, the sweet country! it's glad I shall be to see me pigs again. They won't know me in these glasses!

[*Exit, followed by* MASON.]

STELLA: And now it's time I started for the Wembleys' party. Am I looking my utmost?

LORD BLUEHARNIS: I have seldom seen you looking more so.

MRS CREAMWAY [*rolling up her drawing and the manuscript into a telescope*]: Here is the precious document. It should be left in Fleet Street tonight.

LORD BLUEHARNIS: I will take it myself, now.

MRS CREAMWAY [*slowly*]: There is only one drawback in publishing it, that I can see.

LORD BLUEHARNIS *and* STELLA [*with one voice*]: A drawback?

MRS CREAMWAY: Has it struck you that there may be others who will want to be cured too?

[*A look of consternation creeps into* STELLA'S *face.*]

STELLA: After my marriage I shall only perform miracles on my husband.

LORD BLUEHARNIS: Quite right, and very proper too.

MRS CREAMWAY [*fastening on her wraps and catching up her train over her arm as she goes out*]: I hope, my child, you will not be selfish and neglect your mother.

[*Exit.* STELLA *lingers a moment fussing with her gloves.*]

LORD BLUEHARNIS: Stella, may I? [*They kiss.*]

MRS CREAMWAY [*calling outside*]: Stella! Stella!

LORD BLUEHARNIS [*picking up the account of the miracle, and offering his arm to* STELLA]: Remember, Stella, to write at least twice a day when you are away.

STELLA [*chatting happily as they move towards the door*]: Oh George! I have just remembered the name of such a wonderful photographer in Paris. A Pole! who lives on the tip-top floor down a terrible dark street behind the Morgue. Little Miss Orcas told me about him. She said she fainted with fear—and that was why her eyelashes came out so well. She has warned me when I go, not to leave my maid downstairs in the cab. But you don't know how much I enjoy a shiver, and anything like a warning makes me utterly reckless. [THEY *pass out,* STELLA'S *voice is heard from the staircase growing fainter and fainter:*] I expect after we are married you will discover what a will I have of my own.

[*A moment's silence. Enter* MASON *carrying a gong.* HE *comes forward beating upon it solemnly as might a Eunuch summoning Slaves. Enter* FLORA, *a housemaid.*]

FLORA: Gracious, Mr Mason, what ever is it?

MASON: You may indeed ask! Go down into the basement and summon Mrs Mox when she has put on her black satin, and the rest of the household, including the Pagan Drusilla. There's been doings in this boudoir that will give them food for conversation to their dying day.

FLORA: I am exceedingly sorry to hear it. Who would have thought anything bad of Miss Stella, or of her respectable mother. But there! I've always said that those whose morals seem the most secure, is often the most frail.

MASON [*shocked*]: Hush. Flora Deane! Your mind is polluted by profane literature! No, the saints be praised there have been higher doings than these.

FLORA: I call it wicked of you Mr Mason to whet my curiosity, if nothing of real importance has taken place.

MASON: Then know, there's been a miracle in this boudoir scarcely half an hour ago.

FLORA: How can you say such things, Mr Mason? Where's the cured? [*She looks around expecting to see a body.*]

MASON: Call the rest of the servants, and I will tell you, on the very spot, all I happen to know—No, don't tread between the fireplace and the sofa unless you know yourself to be clean of conscience.

[FLORA *goes out to summon servants, carefully avoiding to pass between the fireplace and the sofa.* MASON *stands corpselike on the hearth rug sounding fancifully harrowing discords upon the gong.*]

CURTAIN SLOWLY

THE
PRINCESS ZOUBAROFF

A COMEDY

DRAMATIS PERSONÆ

ADRIAN SHEIL-MEYER

ERIC TRESILIAN

LORD ORKISH

MONSIGNOR VANHOVE

REGGIE QUINTUS

ANGELO

NADINE SHEIL-MEYER

ENID TRESILIAN

LADY ROCKTOWER

GLYDA, *her daughter*

MARCHESA PITTI-CONTI

DANTE SILVIO PAOLAO, *her son*

MRS NEGRESS

MRS MANGROVE

PRINCESS ZOUBAROFF

ACT I

SCENE I

Florence. Early summer. The garden of the Casa Meyer. Oleanders, giant Ilex, Judas-trees, flowering hibiscus. A few long green palms. In their blue shade a peacock or two. A pillared circle of Bougainvillœa-wreathed arches supporting a hammock R. through which a portion of the house can be seen. Within the circle, a faded-marble statue, representing an effigy of the Virgin Mary, and a miscellaneous array of easy chairs, two or three, and a portable table holding magazines and books, extending down. A rustic arch L. leading to roadway. Distant prospect, Florence. Time, afternoon.

ADRIAN, ERIC

ERIC: Where are they?

ADRIAN: Nadine and Enid have gone hunting together.

ERIC: Hunting?

ADRIAN: For Antiques.

ERIC: Poking round for Antiques—and we've been barely married a week. [ADRIAN *shrugs.*] Our marriage is *manqué!*

ADRIAN: This little jaunt of ours ought to clear the air.

ERIC: Do you know, I believe Enid would be positively glad if I didn't return to her again?

ADRIAN: She seemed quite bright at lunch.

ERIC: Precisely.

ADRIAN [*laughing*]: Between ourselves, I begin to fear we've both made mistakes!

ERIC: I'm glad you can laugh.

ADRIAN: I can't help it.

ERIC: Thank goodness we shall start tomorrow without them.

ADRIAN: Yes. Nadine loathes the Engadine. Mountains depress her nature.

ERIC: Do all mountains?

ADRIAN: Anything she can't see over.

ERIC: Their rarefied atmosphere braces me. I'm never so well as in it.

ADRIAN: It can be had, as well, at home. [*Picking up a book, which he scans.*] "She read romances night and day, and wished to live them, after the fashion of the shepherds of Astrea; she slept upon a sofa painted like grass, and in a room representing trees and sheepfolds; and when the Beloved arrived, she would softly recite the *Eclogues of Fontanelle,* would talk of tender flames the sensitive heart, and dish up all the mawkishness of the Operas."

ERIC: Princess Zoubaroff has been lending *mia moglie* some books.

ADRIAN: One's inclined to be diffident of her influence!

ERIC: Her heart's desire now, I'm told, is to make her Peace with heaven.

ADRIAN: I know of nothing more dangerous; but I can scarcely believe it.

ERIC: One hears strange stories of her—Rumours, in fact.

ADRIAN: She fascinates Nadine and Enid! And here they are.

SCENE II

Same. NADINE SHEIL-MEYER *loaded with bric-à-brac.* ENID TRESILIAN. *Both are ultra beautifully dressed.* MRS SHEIL-MEYER'S *hat is one mass of quivering grasses.*

NADINE: Don't bother.

ENID [*airily helping her*]: An imaginary footman helps.

ADRIAN: What have you been getting?

ENID: Such enthralling things.

ERIC: Let's see.

NADINE: No, no, no, no.

ADRIAN: Peevish!

ENID: She is fagged, I fear, by our expedition.

NADINE [*indignantly*]: I'm not.

ENID: We've been to Ishmael Levy!

ADRIAN: Ah! Beware of fakes.

ENID [*superiorly*]: He offered us a *Lucia Bearing her Eyes upon a Dish* —a supposed original of Masaccio, and a fantastic Moreau like some strong perfume.

ADRIAN: He did?

ENID: A head and hands business.

ADRIAN: Oh?

ENID: And who should there enter as we were glancing round *but Blanche!*

ERIC: Blanche?

ENID: Blanche Negress.

ERIC: Who's she?

ENID: . . . But so charming and so different to the rest!

ERIC: Then she *must* be refreshing.

NADINE: What induced you to ask her here this evening, Enid, by the way?

ENID: Because I thought it might be fun. You know she writes things for the papers.

ADRIAN: What sort of things?

ENID: Oh, don't ask me what sort of things.

NADINE [*throwing her purchases down upon a table*]: She was telling us at the Bretagne they charge her more to board her Great Dane than they do for her maid.

ERIC: Perhaps it eats more!

NADINE: Talking of eating—do you wish for a collation at daybreak before you start?

ADRIAN: No, thanks.

ENID: You're packed?

ERIC: Not quite.

ENID: Could I do anything?

ERIC: It's good of you, dear, but there's practically nothing to do.

NADINE [*inquisitively*]: I suppose you're feeling pleasurably excited at the thoughts of tomorrow?

ERIC: Why not?

ENID: Remember, won't you, Eric, to gather a little Edelweiss if you should notice any.

NADINE: Yes; don't forget that.

ENID: Though no accidents, mind.

NADINE: Naturally.

ERIC [*nettled, his anger rising*]: Say out straight what you mean, can't you?

ENID: What I mean?

ERIC: I don't go in for *arrière pensées.*

ENID: Really, Eric, your hypersensitiveness would try an archangel, I think.

ERIC: Oh! Would it?

NADINE [*disdainfully*]: Poor child, don't mind him! One knows his bow-wow ways.

ENID: I'll not be long, dear [*kissing her finger-tips to her*]. I've a very little letter I must write.

NADINE: Must you?

ENID [*moving towards house*]: Just a few hurried flying lines. . . .

ERIC [*following her*]: And I've some business too! . . .

SCENE III

ADRIAN, NADINE [their *Married* voices]

NADINE: I could laugh when I think of her answering congratulatory letters still!

52

ADRIAN: She's having rather a pale sort of honeymoon apparently.

NADINE: If she's neglected, whose fault is it?

ADRIAN: You surely don't think it's mine!

NADINE: I do.

ADRIAN [*ominously*]: You dare to say that?

NADINE [*with intention*]: Don't let's repeat Egypt!

ADRIAN [*shuddering*]: Not for the universe.

NADINE: He'd better look out. She's just in the mood for fireworks.

ADRIAN: Is she?—the deuce.

NADINE: I know Enid better than Eric. [*Mysteriously:*] She and I were at school together.

ADRIAN: What possessed you to ask her here for her honeymoon?

NADINE [*sentimentally staring at the tip of her shoe*]: Because—I don't know!—I wished to lend her a little support. . . . Chaperone her, so to speak, the difficult first days. Poor darling! She had nobody. She was very unhappy at home.

ADRIAN [*blatantly*]: Eric and I—we too were at school together.

NADINE: Bah! Don't talk to me of Eric.

ADRIAN: He was my friend.

NADINE: What do *I* care?

ADRIAN: You tiresome woman.

NADINE: How dare you call me "tiresome"?

ENID [*returning*]: Excuse me, Nadine, but what is Charlotte's address?

NADINE: Coombe Court, Straithfieldsaye.

ENID: And Elsie?

NADINE: Five Rue Sganarelle. . . .

ENID: Oh, thank you, dear. [*She goes in.*]

NADINE: I can't *bear* to see her look so bored.

ADRIAN: Bored!

NADINE: Poor little soul. It makes one weep to look at her.

ADRIAN: I never saw anyone so . . . [*looking*].

NADINE: What?

ADRIAN: Nothing.

NADINE [*putting up her sunshade*]: I believe you were going to insult her!

ADRIAN [*horror-struck*]: I?

NADINE [*in indignant yet not displeased tones*]: I fancy you were about to say something unkind.

ADRIAN [*pointedly*]: Oh, that I leave to your Florentine friends!

NADINE: To whom do you refer?

ADRIAN [*lighting a cigarette*]: I refer to Lord Orkish. . . .

NADINE: Ah!

ADRIAN: And to Mrs du Wilson. . . .

NADINE: Oh!

ADRIAN: And to Zena Zoubaroff.

NADINE: Zena? But Zena *adores* Enid.

ADRIAN: Rot!

NADINE: She adores her.

[*The garden gate opens and the* PRINCESS ZOUBAROFF, *a very pale, vaguely "sinister-looking" woman of about thirty-five, enters. She wears a riding-habit, rather Vanloo, fringed with sables. In lieu of a riding-crop she holds a fan.*]

PRINCESS: I just looked in to say good-bye!

SCENE IV

ADRIAN, NADINE, PRINCESS

ADRIAN [*gallantly*]: What a charming surprise!

NADINE: We were this moment speaking of you, dear!

PRINCESS [*coming forward*]: Of me? Oh? . . . And what were you saying of me?

NADINE: I was telling Adrian how fond of Enid you seemed.

PRINCESS: How could one help loving her?

ADRIAN [*solicitously*]: Well? And what have *you* been doing?

PRINCESS [*glowing*]: I'm just back from oh, such a heavenly ride. Half-way to Vallombrosa!

NADINE: But wasn't it grilling?

54

ADRIAN [*matter of fact*]: We may expect a storm before morning, I think.

PRINCESS [*drawing off her gloves*]: Rain is needed badly.

NADINE: It would do the young vines good.

ADRIAN: And the garden too. . . .

PRINCESS: Yours is a Paradise. . . . Those purple, tragic roses. . . . Tell me, how are they named?

ADRIAN: I forget.

PRINCESS [*poetically*]: I love the Flowers. They talk to me. I love the Birds. They sing to me!

NADINE: What have they told you—if it's not indiscreet?

PRINCESS [*elusively*]: They say that Opera-cloaks this Spring are going to make one seven good feet across the shoulders.

NADINE: Ah?

PRINCESS: And that sandals shortly are coming in. . . .

NADINE: What else?

PRINCESS [*stooping*]: Let me admire your heliotropes.

ADRIAN [*flatteringly*]: Your own garden, Princess, you know, is all our envy.

PRINCESS [*sighing*]: This year I'm very vain of my pomegranates!

ADRIAN: I don't wonder.

PRINCESS: My beloved garden. You should see it early, at break of day, when Dawn makes its white holes through the trees.

NADINE [*succinctly*]: Perhaps tomorrow they will.

PRINCESS: And so you're really off?

ADRIAN: Yes.

PRINCESS: To those ridiculous mountains?

ADRIAN: Why do you say ridiculous?

PRINCESS: Aren't they?

ADRIAN: Not that I'm aware of.

PRINCESS: I am always disappointed with mountains. There are no mountains in the world as high as I could wish.

ADRIAN: No?

PRINCESS: They irritate me invariably. I should like to shake Switzerland. [*Looks at her hands.*]

NADINE: You have the perfectest hands, Zena.

PRINCESS [*wistfully*]: Have I?

NADINE: You know you have.

PRINCESS: How Ingres admired my hands. He quite worshipped my little fingers.

SCENE V

Same. ENID

ENID: I can't write letters while Eric is fidgeting about.

NADINE [*whispering*]: Wait till we're Alone tomorrow.

ENID: Yes. I think so. Oh, Zena! [*Goes to her.*]

PRINCESS [*regarding her with pensive interest*]: You look done-in, dear; totally done-in.

ENID: Do I?

PRINCESS: Those great fatigued eyes. . . .

NADINE: She does far too much! Last night she was chasing bats after midnight with a long white rosary.

PRINCESS: Have you seen yet all the inevitable sights?

ENID: Oh heavens, no. Beyond a few churches, I've seen nothing whatever.

PRINCESS: Really?

ENID: Imagine, I haven't been at all to the Bargello.

PRINCESS: I was there one morning lately with one of the Hope girls.

ENID: Oh?

PRINCESS: It was dreadful. She would *scream* at everything that attracted her, and fall upon her knees . . . and kiss and touch the things.

NADINE [*with decision*]: I consider the eldest Miss Hope's a disgrace to England! You see her woolgathering about the streets garbed in an old violet velvet sack, her hat set crooked, crammed with flowers.

PRINCESS: Yes! And Tozhy too's a sight.

ENID: Tozhy?

PRINCESS: Mr Hope—the "Father" of the English colony, you know.

ENID: Of course. He is going to show me some time where one can get Venetian glass!

PRINCESS [*leaning on the back of a garden chair*]: I have passed through all the fads, I suppose, myself in furniture and pictures and books. And now all I ask for's a cell. Give me a room with nothing in it!

ENID: How horribly *dull*.

ADRIAN: It must need courage to be so eclectic?

PRINCESS: Not really. [*With vivacity:*] I often think I would rather like to run a Convent.

ENID: Oh, Zena!

PRINCESS: For little girls—not for sour old women.

ADRIAN: Have you remarked the cosmopolitanised faces of the Nuns one meets hereabouts?

PRINCESS: No.

ADRIAN: It's so curious.

PRINCESS [*beating the air dreamily with her fan*]: Florence—I always say it's a place one drifts to in the end!

ADRIAN: It's a pity perhaps so many—what shall I say—people do.

PRINCESS [*with a swift, bright look*]: I hear Reggie Quintus is in the town —looking quite lawless.

ADRIAN: Reggie?

NADINE: Oh!

PRINCESS: Lady Rocktower *saw* him.

NADINE: One would like to be kind to the boy on account of his poor darling mother—but it's a little difficult to, all the same.

PRINCESS [*critically*]: He has the manners of one who has nothing to lose and perhaps something to gain.

NADINE: Perhaps.

PRINCESS: He's so good-looking—too good-looking for a man.

ADRIAN: I don't intend ever having anything to do with him.

PRINCESS: No? Well, perhaps you're wise.

ENID [*looking towards house*]: Why's Eric beckoning?

ADRIAN: I expect he wants his revenge at billiards!

NADINE [*sweetly*]: Go to him, then, won't you, dear? Don't mind us!

ADRIAN: I will.

[*Exit* ADRIAN *to house.*]

SCENE VI

PRINCESS, NADINE, ENID

ENID: This evening I feel so reckless, so reckless. I could wear a forehead-ornament besides a hat!

PRINCESS [*fingering*]: Where did you get that love of a gown?

ENID: It was part of my *corbeille.*

PRINCESS: My dear, you have the instinct for dress. I never saw anything so perfect!

NADINE [*exclaiming*]: Oh! . . .

ENID: Is there anything the matter?

NADINE: What have you done with your wedding ring?

ENID: I took it off.

NADINE: What for?

ENID: I don't mean to wear one.

PRINCESS: But—my dear!

NADINE: Nonsense. You must!

ENID: Why?

NADINE: I insist.

ENID: Oh, of course if you're really keen . . .

PRINCESS: Where is it?

ENID: On the dressing-table in my room.

NADINE: I'll go and find it at once.

[*Exit* NADINE *to house.*]

SCENE VII

PRINCESS, ENID

PRINCESS [*a short silence*]: He has not been cruel?

ENID: No.

PRINCESS: You will make a fatal mistake, dear Enid, if you allow him to go!

ENID [*unconvinced*]: Shall I?

PRINCESS: Remember the Foreign Colony here is a very hornet's nest. . . .

ENID: I can't help it!

PRINCESS [*putting an arm about her*]: How are you with him?

ENID: Since lunch he and I are on tolerable terms again.

PRINCESS: Since lunch? . . .

ENID: After all, it's really rather risible.

PRINCESS: I don't consider it risible in the *very* least.

ENID: Not?

PRINCESS [*emphatic*]: It's an unprecedented honeymoon—*even for Florence!*

ENID: Don't let's grow solemn.

PRINCESS: In my opinion, marriage was something altogether too excessive for such very light desires.

ENID: Desires. . . . [*Smiling wanly:*] Both he and I are dead to any wish.

PRINCESS: Don't say so.

ENID: Ah, but I do.

PRINCESS: What made you accept him, then? Tell me.

ENID: It was purely a match of reason. At home I was generally in the way. Mamma and I were nothing but rivals. But let's not talk about it.

PRINCESS [*retrospective*]: As a raw girl, I'd a disrelish for marriage too. But my parents sensibly made me. And when my first husband died, why, I soon remarried . . . and when he, poor fellow, succumbed—he was a world-renowned explorer—I was induced to listen again. . . . [*Slight pause.*] And I've been married in all *six times!*

ENID [*admiringly*]: What a wonderful accumulation of experience you must have, Zena?

59

PRINCESS: Yes. [*Grimly:*] When I want to impress a stranger, I carry their miniatures on my wrists—three on each arm.

ENID: Your last marriage, was it happy?

PRINCESS: My last marriage, my dear, was one long game of hide-and-seek.

ENID: I feel discouraged!

PRINCESS: A husband, one must remember, is something of an *acquired* taste.

ENID: Are they all alike?

PRINCESS: Why, of course not!

ENID: Aren't they?

PRINCESS [*nibbling her fan*]: No. Really, you provoke me to laugh.

ENID: I've been married a week and it isn't at all what I thought it would be!

PRINCESS [*tenderly*]: Poor darling. How I would love to spoil you.

ENID: You dear. But you do. . . .

PRINCESS: Not enough.

ENID: Oh, Zena!

PRINCESS [*caressing admiringly her hair*]: Not nearly enough, *Elf-locks.*

ENID [*coyly*]: I'm all foolish nerves tonight!

PRINCESS: Poor Angel, Baby, Waif. . . .

ENID [*closing her eyes*]: What would you advise?

PRINCESS: Make the most of youth! Remember nothing lasts. . . .

ENID: You think I should take a lover?

PRINCESS: No, no . . . you'd regret it.

ENID: There's no telling.

PRINCESS: Eventually, of course, you'll build a bridge!

ENID: Impossible.

PRINCESS: Tfoo!

ENID: He's so altered.

PRINCESS: How?

ENID: His tastes!

PRINCESS: They jar?

ENID: Dreadfully. His Hellenism once captivated me. But [*opening her*

60

eyes gloomily as wide as she is able] the *Attic* to him means nothing now
but Servants' bedrooms.

PRINCESS: Servants' what?

ENID [*faintly*]: *Closets.*

PRINCESS [*behind her fan*]: Oh!

ENID: It's revolting.

PRINCESS [*philosophically*]: In life, to be happy, the first rule is to learn
pretty extensively to ignore.

ENID: I suppose, dearest, you were never situated before as I am?

PRINCESS [*nodding*]: Yes, indeed! One of my husbands also left me!

ENID: Oh, Zena?

PRINCESS: Left me even sooner than yours!

ENID: It isn't credible!

PRINCESS: He said a thousand tender pretty things, called me a thousand
charming names. And then, at the end of twenty-four hours, he deserted
me!

ENID: What did you do?

PRINCESS: What could I do?

ENID: If Eric deserts me, I dare say I could start an "Art School" here. It
would be rather fun.

PRINCESS: Darling Enid, anything rather than that!

ENID [*puzzled*]: But why?

PRINCESS: Because . . .

SCENE VIII

Same. NADINE

NADINE [*flourishing wedding ring*]: Here it is!

ENID: Oh, thank you, Nadine.

NADINE: Put it on.

ENID [*evasively*]: It's far too hot to wear a ring!

PRINCESS: Rubbish.

61

NADINE [*suppliant*]: For me, dearest. Say you will!

ENID: Very well then, I will!

PRINCESS [*overbrimming with quiet fun*]: How she dreads a scandal. . . .

NADINE [*her sensitive panic patently subsiding*]: Well, it's not quite pleasant, is it? And foreign servants are such fools! They'd think it was a *faux-ménage,* or something.

ENID: As if I care!

PRINCESS [*urbane*]: Were I she, I'd allow myself, perhaps, a little sneer. . . .

ENID: I don't mean to upset my expression on Eric's account.

PRINCESS: But only a little *tiny* one.

ENID [*toying listlessly with her ring*]: Oh, don't ask me, please, to wear another thing more—! Even a sneer.

PRINCESS: For his good, one could wish he'd some interest. . . . A man should have aspirations, I always contend.

ENID: Ah, there, my dear, I'm with you. When I think that one of Caligula's horses was a Member of Parliament, and when I remember what a plain, simple cow rose to be, I own I'm mortified at Eric's unambition.

PRINCESS [*gasping*]: What did the plain, simple cow rise to be?

ENID: She rose to be an Empress.

NADINE: An Empress?

ENID: Or a Goddess, was it? I'm sure I forget.

[*A piano-organ is heard suddenly beyond the garden gate.*]

NADINE: Horrid to be outdone by animals.

ENID [*to dance air, taking a few tripping steps*]: Well, my dears! It's been a week of wonders!

PRINCESS: What is that?

NADINE [*raising her voice a little because of the organ*]: She says it's been a week of wonders.

PRINCESS: Poor child! A week ago she was an insouciant girl!

NADINE: Insouciant!

PRINCESS [*watching the bride with a mistrustful eye*]: I only hope she won't take to narcotics!

NADINE: We must not let her brood.

[*The organ stops.*]

PRINCESS: One day soon, Enid, let us ride together.

ENID: There's nothing I'd like more, only I've nothing to ride, I'm afraid.

PRINCESS: I will find you a charming little horse.

ENID [*dropping to her knees upon the grass*]: What a darling you are!

PRINCESS [*plying her fan*]: Galloping down some green cattle-track in the cool of evening, child, you will soon forget your worries.

ENID [*nestling*]: Your habit smells of Arcady. . . .

PRINCESS: Of what?

ENID: Arcady.

PRINCESS: Beyond the Porta San Gallo I often dismount and walk.

ENID: Enchanting.

PRINCESS: There's a road bordered by wild acacias I yearn to show you.

ENID [*elated*]: Yes?

PRINCESS: And at its end there's a Calvary . . . and a church designed by Andrea Orcagna with the loveliest windows.

ENID: One might perhaps do a sketch or something?

PRINCESS: The green brightness of the glass is amazingly nice. And such touching mosaics there are. You'll see!

[*Enter through arch* L. LADY ROCKTOWER, *an uncommonly long and lean woman—once a well-known Beauty.*]

SCENE IX

Same. LADY ROCKTOWER

LADY ROCKTOWER [*hand extended, advancing to* NADINE]: I wrote to you about a week ago asking you to dinner, and having received no answer I thought I would ascertain . . .

NADINE [*retaining* LADY ROCKTOWER's *hand captive in her own an instant in token of contrition*]: Did I *never* answer?

LADY ROCKTOWER: Both Lord Rocktower and I will be so disappointed if you fail us tomorrow night!

NADINE: Tomorrow night I fear we shall be without either Adrian or Eric.

LADY ROCKTOWER: Are they leaving Florence?

NADINE: Yes. . . .

LADY ROCKTOWER: Dear me! I didn't know.

NADINE: They're leaving us—and Italy.

LADY ROCKTOWER: I trust nothing serious!

NADINE: Nothing very.

LADY ROCKTOWER: That's right. [*To* ENID:] *My dear,* what a foreign behind! I didn't recognise you at first!

ENID [*amused*]: How do you like my Cinquecento jacket?

LADY ROCKTOWER: Your fastidious, imaginative dresses would not suit everyone.

ENID: Fortunately.

LADY ROCKTOWER [*looking about her*]: Where's Glyda?

NADINE: I don't know!

LADY ROCKTOWER: She came a few yards with me, and suddenly exclaimed: "Oh, bother," and then rushed back.

PRINCESS: Your daughter, I expect, will be here directly.

LADY ROCKTOWER [*shaking hands with* PRINCESS *very cordially*]: Dear Princess! Although you live within a stone's throw, one sees simply *nothing* of you!

PRINCESS: Yes. *How is it,* I wonder?

LADY ROCKTOWER: I don't remember ever having seen you at my *Musicale?*

PRINCESS: Unfortunately. . . . But I hear it was quite wonderful. With Julie Bonbon and Emma Block. . . .

LADY ROCKTOWER: Who told you?

PRINCESS: Mr Waterbird.

LADY ROCKTOWER: I must protest! He wasn't there.

PRINCESS: Oh! . . .

LADY ROCKTOWER: I can't be civil to a political traitor!

NADINE: My dear, in Politics there is no honour. Disraeli has said so.

LADY ROCKTOWER: Anyway I should never invite the Waterbirds. [*Cryptically:*] I regard Mrs Waterbird as *no acquisition!!!*

PRINCESS [*irrelevantly*]: I watched her in the mirror once acting a little pantomime behind my back.

NADINE [*adjusting a pin*]: They say she has three lovers. . . .

PRINCESS: Three?

ENID: Surely three lovers would be very inspiriting!

LADY ROCKTOWER: How is it, I'd like to know, you're parting so soon with yours? Were I a new-made wife, I'd hold my husband tight, grip his coat-tails and not let go!

ENID: His going is of little consequence really.

LADY ROCKTOWER: It's soon to play Penelope yet!

PRINCESS [*a shadow of recollection crossing her face*]: Were I driven to choose, I'd prefer neglect, I think, to surfeit.

LADY ROCKTOWER: That, I suppose, depends upon the man.

PRINCESS [*with a half-laugh*]: A husband's attentions *soon* grow savour-less!

ENID [*her eyes raised towards the Gallery*]: He married me in creaking shoes.

LADY ROCKTOWER: What?

ENID [*reminiscent, unearthly*]: His shoes creaked when he married me!

LADY ROCKTOWER: I conclude you've been catching *glimpses* of each other. . . .

ENID: Glimpses?

LADY ROCKTOWER [*shrewdly*]: I believe this is nothing but a touch of sex-antagonism which presently will pass.

ENID [*evidently pleased with the consequence of the situation*]: This morning my maid found three little grey ones—hairs.

NADINE [*sympathetically*]: Darling Enid! She talks like an old woman and she's a mere *fillette* still!

LADY ROCKTOWER: Were I you, my dear, I would go for him tooth-and-nail!

PRINCESS [*conciliatory*]: I always pour oil on troubled waters. Harmony for me.

ENID [*with importance*]: Three little grey ones. . . .

[*She goes up stage enumerating them upon her fingers, and disappears after a moment in the garden.*]

NADINE [*following her with a look*]: Now she has gone off into some jewelled Hades of her own.

LADY ROCKTOWER: I'm bewildered to know what to advise!

NADINE [*musingly*]: It's difficult to interfere—Enid and Eric vying in vanity with each other as they do.

LADY ROCKTOWER: They're not sufficiently different, one feels, to be happy together.

PRINCESS: Enid's clever of course but she needs directing.

LADY ROCKTOWER [*irreflective*]: One comfort is there's no issue!

PRINCESS: My dear, give them time!

NADINE: It's quite dreadful to hear her refer to her wedding day as *Black Tuesday.*

LADY ROCKTOWER: Thank Heaven! Marriage isn't indissoluble.

PRINCESS: They're unreckonably temperamental. Both of them. . . .

LADY ROCKTOWER: People of their sort oughtn't to marry.

NADINE: Last night she had a bad *crise des nerfs* and began calling sixteen "the Old Age of Youth."

PRINCESS [*fluttering her fan*]: Is she *only* sixteen?

NADINE [*ignoring the interruption*]: So this morning I sent into town for Dr Mater.

LADY ROCKTOWER: I don't think much of Dr Mater. He'll tell you of all sorts of things to avoid, things that *in any case* it would never occur to one to take!

PRINCESS: What did he say?

NADINE: He has ordered her milk and the wings of chickens.

[*Enter* GLYDA ROCKTOWER, *aged eleven. She is pale, plump, precocious— an attaching manner.*]

SCENE X

Same. GLYDA

PRINCESS: Ah! . . . *ecco la!*

LADY ROCKTOWER: Wicked peach.

GLYDA [*standing legs apart and swinging insolently her skirts*]: I met some people in the lane.

LADY ROCKTOWER: Who?

GLYDA: Guess?

LADY ROCKTOWER: I can't.

GLYDA [*pirouetting, preening herself*]: Apollo—and Lord Orkish.

LADY ROCKTOWER: Apollo—who?

GLYDA: Reggie Quintus.

LADY ROCKTOWER: Oh!

GLYDA: I told them you were here. They're coming in.

[*Enter* LORD ORKISH. *He is, despite "Exile" and a "certain age," all cheerfulness, gaiety and sweet good-humour. Behind him* REGGIE QUINTUS. *Incredibly young. Incredibly good-looking. No one would suppose him to have figured as hero already in at least one* cause célèbre—*his manner, which is somewhat "subdued," alternates between the demi-dazed and the demi-demure.*]

SCENE XI

Same. LORD ORKISH, REGGIE QUINTUS

LORD ORKISH: Do we intrude?

NADINE: Delighted.

LORD ORKISH: We've just been paying a *visite de digestion* on Comtesse Willie White, and are on our way to Salut at San Lorenzo.

NADINE: Then there's no immediacy, is there?

LORD ORKISH [*shaking hands*]: Why, none.

LADY ROCKTOWER: Perhaps you can inform me if Madame Gandarella is still at the Villa?

LORD ORKISH: Yes; and Santuzza.

NADINE [*laughing*]: That poor Santuzza. She has the most fearful English accent in the world. Where is it! What is it! Who could have taught her? I wonder.

LORD ORKISH: People are circulating such dreadful stories!

PRINCESS [*miraculously*]: What about?

LORD ORKISH: I'm so newsy. [*Irrepressibly:*] I feel I must tell it to some-body, if only a lizard, or a butterfly, or a garden-snail!

NADINE: Sit down and tell us instead.

[*All but imperceptibly, twilight begins to form.*]

LORD ORKISH: I've but just this afternoon heard the Alpmuriels are leaving one another! . . . Mrs Alpmuriel, in fact, has already gone.

LADY ROCKTOWER, NADINE: Gone? [*Ensemble:*] Where?

LORD ORKISH: Away.

LADY ROCKTOWER: Dear me!

LORD ORKISH [*impressionistically*]: Instead of surprising them—*comment dirai-je?*—he found them, unmysteriously eating.

LADY ROCKTOWER: *Eating?*

LORD ORKISH: Only imagine!!! And he with his drawn sword—or a re-volver, was it?

LADY ROCKTOWER: Oh!

LORD ORKISH [*playing extinct eyes*]: Sir Dolfin Lewis is defending her.

PRINCESS [*amused*]: And what else, Lord Orkish, did you hear at the Villa White?

LORD ORKISH: That the new American Ambassadress likes to be thought a little *grisette*.

LADY ROCKTOWER: I sat next her a short while ago at the Teatro Valli.

NADINE: You did not tell me you had been to Rome!

REGGIE [*in a voice which is rather like cheap scent*]: Perhaps you won't agree. But I consider Florence has fewer amenities than Rome.

NADINE: It depends what one means by amenities, quite.

REGGIE [*regarding thoughtfully his white compact hands*]: I always feel a sort of *malaise* in Florence. Why, I can't tell.

LADY ROCKTOWER [*austerely*]: I fear the morals of the town are not especially high!

LORD ORKISH: A neighbour of ours sent her little maid the other night across the Piazza for a bottle of French brandy, and she has not been heard of again.

NADINE: How dreadful.

ENID [*coming down with a watering-can of Pesaro pottery in her hand. She is smiling and has tucked into her dress a huge blue Passion-flower*]: I heard men's voices. . . .

NADINE: Lord Orkish has been regaling us with a whole rosary of piquant anecdotes.

ENID: Really.

NADINE [*to* LORD ORKISH]: You've such wonderful *entraînement.*

LORD ORKISH [*very simply*]: I'm never bored. I enjoy everything.

REGGIE: So do I too! I love society. Alone with my shadow I'm soon depressed.

NADINE [*rather nervously*]: And where have you been to, Reggie, this perfect age?

REGGIE [*bending his head a little on one side to inhale the scent of the tuberose flowers that are in his button-hole*]: I and a friend of mine, Claud Cloudley, we've been visiting all the P's.

NADINE: All the what?

REGGIE: Pavia, Parma, Padua, Perugia, Pisa—

PRINCESS: Is it a method?

REGGIE: Claud's such an extremist, you know. [*Lowering impressively his voice:*] They say when he kissed the Pope's slipper [*a gentle cough*] he went on to do considerably *more.* . . .

GLYDA [*intrigued*]: What's he like, Reggie?

REGGIE [*nonchalantly*]: He's rather good-looking in a sickly sort of way.

GLYDA [*disappointed*]: What a description!

ENID [*slyly*]: I expect he's very good-looking!

REGGIE [*smiling*]: He's sickly.

PRINCESS: I remember him coming to see me once in England, with his dripping umbrella.

LORD ORKISH: Shall you be going to England, Princess, later on?

PRINCESS [*cooling her cheeks with a powder-puff*]: Perhaps, if I can afford it.

NADINE: To hear her speak, she might be a Poor Clare!

LADY ROCKTOWER [*vivaciously*]: Our villa is let for the coming villeggia-tura to Madame Olga Wittena-Gemot, the famous singer, and my husband is rampant with me because Renaldo Renetti—

[*Re-enter* ERIC, *with billiard cue.*]

SCENE XII

Same. ERIC

ERIC [*to* ENID]: Shake me a cocktail, darling. Do.

ENID: Oh, don't ask me to do anything so violent, Eric. Where's Angelo?

NADINE [*who looks as though she would be also glad of some refresh-ment herself*]: What shall it be? West-Coast? Manhattan? Kiss-me-Quick?

ERIC: Let it be a Gloom-Raiser.

NADINE: There's no more absinthe, I fear.

ERIC: Then a Champagne-Cobbler.

NADINE [*generally*]: Will you excuse me?

[*Exit* NADINE *to house.*]

LADY ROCKTOWER: Now, I'm going to scold him!

ENID: No, Lady Rocktower.

LADY ROCKTOWER: And Princess Zoubaroff shall second me.

PRINCESS: Oh, please! I'm unrepresented. [*She drifts away.*]

ERIC: *Buona sera.*

[*He begins balancing his billiard cue in the palm of his hand.* ENID, *with an ironic glance, follows* PRINCESS *towards hammock, where* LORD ORKISH *and* REGGIE *have commenced rocking* GLYDA.]

ENID [*witheringly, withdrawing*]: He is the Eternal-masculine.

LADY ROCKTOWER [toute entière à sa proie attachée]: Heartless man; and so you're going to leave us?

ERIC [*inconsequently*]: For a time.

LADY ROCKTOWER: You propose, of course, returning?

ERIC [*with an air of detachment*]: I expect so!

LADY ROCKTOWER: I think Enid is a saint about it all. [*Warming:*] For a honeymoon's a honeymoon, however one looks at it.

ERIC: Bored people do desperate things.

LADY ROCKTOWER [*fairly floored*]: Why on earth did you marry?

ERIC [*ceasing juggling*]: I was only half-serious when I proposed.

LADY ROCKTOWER: And she accepted you?

ERIC: I never expected to be taken quite *au pied de la lettre.*

LADY ROCKTOWER: Fool.

ERIC: I beg your pardon?

LADY ROCKTOWER: I said insensate! [*He continues his experiments with the cue.*] [*Beside herself:*] Come down to us a little more. Forsake those heights!

ERIC [*turning away*]: If I leave you for a moment will you forgive me?

ENID [*reapproaching*]: Lady Rocktower! Please—

LADY ROCKTOWER: He seems determined!

ENID: Let him go.

LADY ROCKTOWER [*susceptibly*]: He has nice eyes.

ENID: There's something agreeably piquant—*almost*—about his excessive leanness!

LADY ROCKTOWER: Perhaps so.

ENID: And I don't so *much* detest his big, bold nose!

LADY ROCKTOWER: Tell me, dear. Were you solicited besides?

ENID: Was I—

LADY ROCKTOWER: Did anyone else ask you?

ENID [*exaggerating*]: I should say so indeed. I might have married whom I liked.

LADY ROCKTOWER: You seem to have selected an enigma!

ENID [*playing with her Passion-flower*]: I will say this for Eric, he isn't carnal.

LADY ROCKTOWER: He isn't carnal enough, my dear, from what *I* can see. [*Half to herself:*] He must have the blood of an Esquimau!

ENID: I scarcely realised, I suppose, at the time of my marriage, I was taking him on for a *term of years.*

LADY ROCKTOWER [*prophetic*]: Oh! But it won't be years! A term of weeks, dear, more like at the rate things go.

ENID: I think my nerves need Mozart.

[*Enter* ANGELO, *a boy of sixteen, fair, sleek, languishing, a "Benozzo Gozzoli," bearing a tray with lemonade, sorbets, fruit, etc. He wears a trim black livery with violet-coloured facings and shoulder-knots.*]

SCENE XIII

Same. ANGELO

LADY ROCKTOWER [*helping herself recklessly to strawberries*]: I will order a Novena said for you.

[*Attracted by* ANGELO *and the tinkle of ice,* GLYDA *and* REGGIE *come down, followed more leisurely by* LORD ORKISH *and* PRINCESS. *Later* NADINE. *The twilight deepens. Lights, here and there, shine from town.*]

REGGIE: I believe strawberries are the clue to my heart!

ENID: Are they?

REGGIE: I'm most awfully *friand* of fruit.

GLYDA [*circling butterfly about*]: I'm fond of grapes, and apricots if they're green. . . . I can't say I like *bananas.*

LADY ROCKTOWER: Fastidious child.

REGGIE: I adore them.

GLYDA: How much?

REGGIE [*wittily*]: As a Russian does Nice.

ENID: Angelo! [*Backing him down towards footlights.*]

ANGELO: Signora!

ENID [*sotto voce*]: Have you the key of your master's valise?

ANGELO [*passionately*]: Ah, Madonna!

ENID: Answer me.

ANGELO [*as before*]: Ah, Mamma mia!

ENID [*taking a sorbet*]: You haven't?

ANGELO: Ah, caro Dio!

ENID: It doesn't matter.

ANGELO: Ah, che roba! [*He crosses stage, rolling his black eyes, passing* ADRIAN L.]

SCENE XIV

Same. ADRIAN

ADRIAN [*to* ENID]: Have you seen Eric?

ENID [*sipping her sorbet*]: He was here a moment ago.

ADRIAN: Visitors! [*He seems disconcerted at sight of* REGGIE.]

PRINCESS [*continuing her conversation with* LORD ORKISH]: I sent my new photo quarter-face to the Cardinal, and he said—

ENID [*drinking still*]: You'll think of the Edelweiss, won't you—if it's only a single sprig!

ADRIAN: Eh?

ENID: It would so touch Nadine . . . Poor angel. She's always wanting some rare, far thing.

ADRIAN: I know.

ENID [*lightly*]: So be, be a dear!

REGGIE [*deftly, to* LADY ROCKTOWER, *without interrupting at all* ADRIAN *and* ENID]: They had hoped it was Tiepolo—but it's only Sebastian Ricci.

ADRIAN: But it isn't the season for Edelweiss.

ENID: Nonsense!

ADRIAN: I promise you.

ENID: You needn't try to put me off with an excuse!

LORD ORKISH [*very deftly, to* PRINCESS]: Lady Audrey's still at Cannes. I hear you wouldn't know her! She's grown so stout.

ENID [*asserting her voice pathetically in general appeal*]: Isn't it the season for Edelweiss?

LADY ROCKTOWER: For Edelweiss? I'm sure I don't know.

ENID [*setting down her glass*]: It is the season. It *is.*

GLYDA [*to* PRINCESS]: What is the music written on your fan?

PRINCESS: A gipsy song—a *chansonnette.*

ENID [*obstinately*]: I will wager you what you like, Edelweiss grows *all the year round.*

NADINE [*re-entering from house*]: I think I hear the front door bell!

ADRIAN: It's amazing you hear anything.

[*Enter* ANGELO, *followed by* BLANCHE.]

ANGELO [*announcing*]: Mrs Negress. [*He goes out, looking over his shoulder, apparently at* REGGIE.]

SCENE XV

Same. BLANCHE NEGRESS. *Her hair, worn short, in wildest spirals, is tinged with white. She is dressed in grey, like a Béguine. She has a pannier of red lilies.*

BLANCHE: I walked along a pink footpath, through the olive-gardens till I saw a dog, which *nearly* drove me back. I don't know why it should be, but Italian dogs fly at me as a rule!

ENID [*accepting pannier, which* BLANCHE *tends*]: It's nice, your coming.

NADINE: Do you know everybody? Lady Rocktower, Mrs Negress—Lord Orkish, Mr Quintus, Princess Zoubaroff—Zena, this is Blanche!

PRINCESS: Delighted.

LORD ORKISH: I expect it was *my* dog. I left one at the door. [*He moves up.*]

NADINE [*introducing*]: My husband.

BLANCHE [*genially*]: I think we've slept together once?

ADRIAN: I don't remember.

BLANCHE: At the Opera. During *Bérénice!*

ADRIAN: Why, of course.

NADINE [*glimpsing* ERIC]: Mr Tresilian—

ERIC: I give you full permission to slay me.

ENID: Why should she wish to slay you?

NADINE: Hark to his guilty conscience!

PRINCESS [*to* BLANCHE]: I confess, with shame, I never read one of your books.

BLANCHE [*amiable*]: It took me four years to choose my *nom de guerre* —Mary.

PRINCESS [*with a cry*]: Are you Mary?

74

BLANCHE: I am.

PRINCESS: Oh, then, *Love's Visée*—I know. . . . And *Lesbia, or Would He Understand?* [*Her admiration is boundless.*]

ENID [*indicating books*]: By the way, Zena, I haven't thanked you properly—

PRINCESS: Were any of them interesting at all?

ENID: I should think so.

PRINCESS [*affectionately*]: *Cara.*

ENID [*with a look at* ERIC]: I'm glad I can still sometimes drug my senses with a book.

NADINE: I've been perusing *Lord Tiredstock's Memoirs.*

PRINCESS: His biography is the barest memoranda, but it's wonderful.

[REGGIE, *at table where are* PRINCESS's *books, chuckles.*]

ENID: What is amusing you?

REGGIE [*convulsed*]: *Orfeo.*

ENID: What about it?

REGGIE: It's too cruel.

ENID: No.

REGGIE [*reading*]: "Woman is an object that always makes man ridiculous."

NADINE [*shrieking*]: Fiend!

REGGIE [*continuing*]: "If she is ugly—oh! What a misery! If she is beautiful—oh! What a danger! And whether one takes her or leaves her one always repents one's action."

LADY ROCKTOWER [*protesting*]: Well, really!

ENID: Aren't you ashamed to read such things aloud to *us?*

REGGIE: You said I might.

PRINCESS: Mercifully, very soon it will be too dark to read!

GLYDA [*indicating*]: Oh, do look at the sky!

NADINE: Extravagant, isn't it?

ERIC [*grumbling*]: Another airless night!

LADY ROCKTOWER: I'm quite glad, do you know, of my Risorgimento cape. [*Puts wrap on.*]

PRINCESS: It is lightening a little towards the town.

BLANCHE: Florence fascinates me at sundown with its scores of shimmering lights.

LADY ROCKTOWER: The evenings grow dark here so very beautifully.

GLYDA: There's a sickle moon.

PRINCESS: Where? Show me.

GLYDA: Can't you see it? There, through the trees. [*She turns to* BLANCHE.]

BLANCHE [*modestly*]: I fear I'm becoming too obese to look at the moon.

ADRIAN [*inviting*]: Then look, do, at the shadows instead.

BLANCHE [*staring*]: The shadows?

NADINE: Adrian sees shapes in everything. [*Laughing:*] He calls the trees at the foot of the garden an "obscene brigade."

LADY ROCKTOWER: My dear, if they choose to grow that way . . .

PRINCESS [*indolently*]: Not a frond stirs. It's as if a spell held all fast.

ENID [*sniffing*]: Delicious. The fresh odour of the dew.

PRINCESS: My favourite tree is certainly the Cypress.

GLYDA [*taking her fan from her and using it*]: Why?

PRINCESS: It tells no tales!

NADINE: But monotonous, like all evergreens are.

BLANCHE [*blinking at a flash of summer lightning*]: There was a beautiful thunderstorm the evening I arrived.

ENID: At the "Bretagne," Blanche, you would see!

BLANCHE: Yes; my room is on the river.

LORD ORKISH [*returning*]: I don't know at all what the Arno is coming to. I was leaning on my window-sill [*laughs*] and there were some youths who appeared to be bathing without false modesty of *any* kind.

LADY ROCKTOWER [*covering her eyes with an elaborately becoroneted Vanity-bag*]: How dreadful.

LORD ORKISH [*pursuing*]: I'm sure if I looked it was quite involuntary.

LADY ROCKTOWER [*sympathetically*]: I'm sure you couldn't help yourself from standing and looking.

NADINE [*sentimentally*]: I love the Arno at low water.

ADRIAN: It's always that. Beyond the town it's unnavigable for even a newspaper!

ERIC [*to* BLANCHE]: Enid was saying you write for one.

BLANCHE [*proudly*]: I write for several.

ERIC: Oh? Which?

BLANCHE: Mainly women's. . . . [*A little sadly:*] I was instrumental *in a very large degree* in obtaining my sex the vote.

PRINCESS: You are one of our champions then?

BLANCHE: Yes.

LADY ROCKTOWER: I'm glad you believe in us!

BLANCHE: Men amuse me sometimes. [*Simply:*] But I have never really loved one.

ERIC [*astonished*]: You have never loved *any* man?

BLANCHE: Never!

LADY ROCKTOWER [*nervously fastening a hook to her cape*]: It's a pleasure to meet now and again a woman of really advanced morals.

BLANCHE: I can safely say I prefer the society of other women to that of men.

PRINCESS: That's nice of you.

LADY ROCKTOWER [*to* NADINE]: Well, dear, I really must run. I wish I hadn't had to!

NADINE: Must you?

ENID: Stay a little while. It's absurdly early yet.

LADY ROCKTOWER: There's to be a small *sauterie* this evening at the Harkovs'.

NADINE: We were asked, but I didn't feel like going.

ENID: I'm far too slack to go fagging up to Fiesole tonight.

LADY ROCKTOWER [*to* GLYDA]: Come, child!

NADINE: Good-bye. You'll come and see me sometimes, won't you?

LADY ROCKTOWER [*moving towards garden gate with* GLYDA]: Often, if you wish it.

ENID: Do!

LADY ROCKTOWER [*up stage, at a distance*]: Tomorrow . . . let me see. Is there no charming church where we could go and sit?

SCENE XVI

Same. Minus LADY ROCKTOWER *and* GLYDA

LORD ORKISH [*low, to* REGGIE]: And we ought to be toddling too.

REGGIE [*deaf, to* ERIC]: We might frivol round together one evening if you like.

ERIC [*primly*]: I should love to, only I've no leisure for anything just now.

PRINCESS [*observant, to* LORD ORKISH]: In Spain, I'm told, you must first court the husband to get round the wife.

LORD ORKISH [*appalled at so much cynicism*]: Madame! Madame?

BLANCHE [*to* ADRIAN, *designating something*]: What is that big brick pile?

ADRIAN [*looking*]: Where? You surely don't mean the Signoria?

BLANCHE: Such a sad, fateful sunset.

LORD ORKISH [*touching* REGGIE's *arm*]: Ready?

REGGIE [*backing out of Salut*]: I'm so sorry . . . but I clean forgot! I've a *rendez-vous.*

LORD ORKISH: Where?

REGGIE: At the quag end of the Cascine.

LORD ORKISH: Which end's that?

REGGIE: The quag end? The far end. . . .

LORD ORKISH: We can go part of the way together.

NADINE [*coming down*]: Dear Lady Rocktower. She gets statelier every year. [*Seeing* LORD ORKISH *and* REGGIE *are preparing to depart:*] What? You're off?

LORD ORKISH: It's getting late.

NADINE: Try and look in tomorrow.

REGGIE [*to* PRINCESS]: Bye-bye. I press your hand. [*Does so.*]

LORD ORKISH: I fear I'm engaged tomorrow.

NADINE: Tiresome creature!

LORD ORKISH [*as he goes up, accompanied by* REGGIE]: I'm attending a tertulia *chez Camille!*

NADINE [*graciously*]: Well, *addio* for the present.

78

[*Exeunt, by garden gate,* LORD ORKISH *and* REGGIE.]

BLANCHE [*precipitately making after them*]: As they know the way, I think I'll go with them.

[*Exit* BLANCHE.]

SCENE XVII

Same. Minus LORD ORKISH, REGGIE, BLANCHE

PRINCESS: It must be almost dinner-time!

ADRIAN: I expect you're hungry after riding so far.

PRINCESS: I am!

ERIC: That's right.

PRINCESS: This morning my French cook got locked, by mistake, in the orchid-house, and I've had nothing to eat all day.

NADINE *and* ENID [*coming down*]: Stay and dine with us.

PRINCESS: Impossible.

ENID: Because?

PRINCESS: I must change.

NADINE: Look in after, then.

ENID: Yes, do, Zena.

PRINCESS [*considering*]: Perhaps I may peep in quite at the very end of the evening.

NADINE: We'll expect you.

PRINCESS [*going*]: I'll bring a little volume of Higher Mystician with me—shall I?—that I think you'll *adore.*

ENID [*blowing her a kiss*]: How delightful.

PRINCESS: Till by-and-by.

[*Exit* PRINCESS.]

SCENE XVIII

ADRIAN, ERIC, NADINE, ENID

ADRIAN [*to* ERIC]: Shall we finish our game?

ERIC: By all means.

ENID [*affronted*]: Are you going indoors?

ERIC [*with simpering ardour*]: *Auf Wiedersehen,* my deathless girl.

[*Exeunt* ADRIAN *and* ERIC.]

SCENE XIX

NADINE, ENID

ENID [*complaining*]: Why aren't the Nightingales singing, and why is there no moon?

NADINE: But there is, dearest. A delicate new one—all for us.

ENID: I mean a proper moon.

NADINE: My dear Enid [*focusing the moon with a black-rimmed eyeglass*], I see nothing improper about this one.

ENID: I meant a full moon, darling.

NADINE: I don't know why you should prefer it to be full. A full moon is perhaps rather vulgar!

ENID: Vulgar?

NADINE: Just a little.

[ANGELO *enters and takes away empty glasses, murmuring intermittently to himself below his breath.*]

ANGELO: *Ah poveretta! La povera signora. Ah che roba! Ah, Dio!* [*He is almost crying in his distress for* ENID.]

ENID: I suppose they leave early?

NADINE: I've no idea.

ENID: I shan't come down.

NADINE: Neither will I. I intend receiving his parting peck in bed.

ENID: Eric never gives me such tangible proofs of his affection.

NADINE: Doesn't he?

ENID: In the morning he just touches my hand—and then he just grazes it—*et encore!!*—again at night.

NADINE [*after an instant, pacing to and fro*]: You know, Enid, I consulted Dr Mater this morning, after he'd seen you.

ENID: What about?

NADINE [*after another instant*]: My health is in a very delicate state, dear.

ENID [*alarmed*]: Darling Nadine!

NADINE: Yes, I may be obliged—but I won't tax your little ears with it just now.

ENID [*anxious to ascertain the facts*]: Is it anything dreadful?

NADINE: It depends what one means quite by dreadful. [*Half-hysterically:*] Define dreadful!

ENID [*taking* NADINE's *hand*]: I'm so sorry . . .

NADINE [*turning from her*]: Of course we may all be wrong. . . .

ENID [*with fervour*]: I do sincerely hope so!

NADINE: I must go and dress. . . .

ENID [*calling after her*]: Tell Fergusson, dear, as you're going in, my gown with the Camellias.

SCENE XX

ENID, *sola. She stands a moment, lost in conjecture. All the bells of Florence ring out. From the Judas-tree a nightingale utters a trill. Another replies. . . . All in an instant the air is full of the singing of birds, the tintinnabulation of bells. The sky is abloom with stars.*

ENID [*to herself, aloud*]: What can she be going to have?

[*Moving towards a flower-plat she inhales, indolently, a flower. A gong goes within. Right hand to hip, left raised to chevelure, she goes slowly up.*]

81

ENID [*lifting roguishly towards the sky her face*]: It sounds almost as though she were sickening for the Plague. . . .

THE CURTAIN FALLS

ACT II

Same as Act I, only the trees have changed their tints. Some are orange, some are scarlet. Red creepers. Autumn flowers.

NADINE, *slightly overdressed in black, with a colossal hat of Piedmontese cock's feathers, is seen with a couple of lace pocket-handkerchiefs tied to two fingers (which she bobs and waggles), diverting her infant son.* ENID, *from hammock (her gown is white, with clusters of sophisticated-looking fruit hanging from it), is listlessly watching her.*

ENID [*breaking at last the "September Silence"*]: Why did you have it?

NADINE [*with a sigh, half of pride, half of resignation*]: My dear, I simply couldn't help myself. . . .

ENID: I thought you cleverer!

NADINE [*to the infant*]: Charles Augustus Frederic Humphrey Percy Sydney!

ENID: At any rate, I'm glad the christening's over.

NADINE [*soulfully*]: Yes. But it was beautiful.

ENID [*despondently*]: And now this wretched party.

NADINE [*kissing little* CHARLES]: He is just like an opening orchid.

ENID [*sitting up—she has in her hand a crystal*]: Just like what?

NADINE [*rocking*]: Forgive a mother's selfishness.

ENID: I won't let him monopolise you, Nadine.

NADINE [*oblivious*]: His mania for pulling everything to pieces makes me anxious for his happiness later on.

83

ENID [*looking round*]: Here is Mrs Mangrove.

[*Enter* NURSE. *She is Scotch. Portly. A woman of fifty. One realises imme-diately she would have her theories, her "little ways," as regards Nursery matters.*]

SCENE II

Same. NURSE

NADINE: You shall take him, Nurse.

NURSE: Very good, marm. [*Taking child.*]

NADINE: Gently, mind.

NURSE [*bursting into song*]:

> The man in the moone drinks claret,
> Eates powdered beef, turnip and caret,
> But a cup of old Malaga sack
> Will fire the bushe at his backe.

ENID [*detached*]: I hope you enjoyed the christening, Nurse?

NURSE: To be sure. I seldom saw a bonnier.

NADINE [*privately, to* NURSE]: See that he—

NURSE: He doesn't want to again, marm, Lord bless you! [*She bustles off through the trees with the child nevertheless.*]

SCENE III

NADINE, ENID

NADINE [*distressed*]: I am afraid she cannot have seen very distinguished service.

ENID: In the last family that she was in, on Notting Hill, she told me the governess and the five children used to go out roller-skating through the London streets. . . .

84

NADINE [*crossing over to her*]: Have you made any further discovery, Enid, in the crystal at all?

ENID: It's difficult. . . . I ought to have something to hold.

NADINE [*drawing something from her dress*]: Here is the last letter he wrote to me.

ENID [*taking it*]: Thanks.

NADINE: I feel it may be the last he *ever* wrote. . . .

ENID [*airily*]: Something tells me they are the two that slipped.

NADINE [*closing her eyes, gesticulating*]: It's appalling to think of them both falling . . . sinking.

ENID: Tsch!

NADINE: You may read what Adrian says.

ENID [*humouring her*]: "The walks—the walks are a continual delight. On all sides—turn where one will—beauty breaks on beauty. . . ."

NADINE [*euphoniously, with her lips*]: Beauty breaks on beauty. . . .

ENID [*resuming*]: "Wonder leaps on wonder" [*her voice breaking a little*]. "I think of you sometimes at Livorno, where the green waves roll in ceaselessly and the brown fishing-nets upon the beach lie drying in the sun."

NADINE: Because I told him we might be going to Livorno.

ENID [*commenting*]: A more depraved-looking autograph I've seldom seen!

NADINE [*with authority*]: Now use the ball.

ENID [*after an instant*]: In the crystal I see a beautiful little giraffe.

NADINE: A giraffe?

ENID: Such a darling. Oh, and I can see a hut, a little house. . . .[*She begins to squeal.*]

NADINE: That must be the guide's dwelling.

ENID [*still gazing*]: I think it's an antelope, not a giraffe.

NADINE [*anxiously*]: What is it doing?

ENID [*straining*]: Nothing.

NADINE: There, that's enough for the present, I want you fresh for the party.

ENID [*returning letter*]: It's a mistake, I think, having ordered tea indoors.

NADINE: It saves a lot of bother.

ENID [*thoughtfully*]: Awkward if Monsignor Vanhove should call here today.

NADINE [*flurried, applying to her lips a cosmetic*]: Did Zena say he'd call?

ENID: She said he might.

NADINE: I believe she intends taking it.

ENID: What? The veil?

NADINE: I'm sure.

ENID [*thrilled*]: But *are* you?

NADINE: And what's more, my dear, she also intends us!

ENID [*giggling nervously*]: Oh, I could never be a nun.

NADINE: Couldn't you?

ENID: Could I? . . .

[*Enter* PRINCESS.]

NADINE: Ah, here is Charlie's new godmother.

SCENE IV

Same. PRINCESS. *She wears something which is crocus-coloured, contrasting radiantly with the autumnal foliage of the trees, a foppish hat, a winter-day muff. . . . She is looking charmingly Carthaginian.*

PRINCESS [*coming forward*]: Charles Augustus Frederic—what are the others?

NADINE: Humphrey, Percy, Sydney.

PRINCESS [*frowning, shocked*]: Such a wicked, dissolute name!

ENID: Names. . . .

NADINE: *Cher amour.*

PRINCESS: Well, Charlie's mother [*taking NADINE's hands*], you're happy? You're content?

NADINE [*soulful, ethereal as before*]: It was beautiful.

ENID [*matter of fact*]: Was Violet du Wilson present?

PRINCESS [*nodding*]: With a sort of Starfish in her hair.

86

NADINE: Violet's changed. She has the look of a great sinner. . . .

PRINCESS: Poor little woman—I want her *so* much.

NADINE [*dropping her eyes*]: You want her? What for?

PRINCESS: For my community.

ENID: Oh, Zena!

PRINCESS: I want you too.

NADINE: Us?

PRINCESS: I mean to have you.

ENID: No.

PRINCESS [*giving* ENID *a brush in the face with her muff*]: Oh, yes I do.

ENID [*changing the subject*]: Who else did you see at Santa Maria Novella?

PRINCESS [*vaguely*]: The Harkovs, the Scharas, the Rocktowers. [*Laughing:*] Even old Mr Hope, who never goes anywhere. . . .

NADINE: I can't suffer Countess Harkov, I'm afraid. She thinks she has only to smile to stir up an ocean of passion.

PRINCESS: It's a pity now she's getting to look so bloated.

ENID [*meaningly*]: You don't want her, I hope!

PRINCESS [*Christian*]: I want everybody—at least—

ENID [*curiously*]: But have you found your site?

PRINCESS [*mysteriously*]: I'm in communication with the Vatican now.

NADINE: So you are actually in touch!

PRINCESS [*nodding*]: My prospectus, I may say, is practically approved. . . .

ENID: By the Holy Father?

PRINCESS [*evasively*]: Monsignor Vanhove would do anything for me.

NADINE: Where will you fix?

PRINCESS: Beyond Settignano, I think.

ENID: Zena!

PRINCESS: What?

ENID: It's too utterly Uganda.

PRINCESS: Uganda?

ENID: Far off.

PRINCESS: Nonsense . . . what does one want to be near to?

ENID [*racily*]: I don't know what one wants to be near, but I know that Settignano is dreadfully ungetatable.

PRINCESS: One can't attain soul-stillness, dearest, within earshot of trains and trams.

NADINE [*catching her infant's howl*]: No, nor within earshot of my son and heir!

[*Exit* NADINE *hurriedly to house.*]

SCENE V

ENID, PRINCESS

ENID [*hands to ears*]: *Should I, could I, might I, dare I,* drown it?

PRINCESS [*by hammock, frankly smiling*]: I almost wish you could.

ENID [*shocked, surprised*]: How ungodmotherly, Zena, of you!

PRINCESS [*seating herself*]: The worst of it is the Holy Father may not consent to have a boy brought up among us. . . .

ENID [*wondering, artless*]: Among whom?

PRINCESS: A little girl would have been easier to receive. . . .

ENID: Where?

PRINCESS: In a Religious House.

ENID [*laughing*]: A young man of Charlie's age can go anywhere.

PRINCESS [*scrupulous*]: It might give the nuns thoughts.

ENID [*still laughing*]: Thoughts?

PRINCESS [*toying with the tassels on her muff*]: Sexual ones.

ENID: Oh . . . but an infant!

PRINCESS: All the same, dear, infants—and a nun is such a sensitive creature as a rule.

ENID: I can't see that it matters at all. [*After a hesitation:*] It might do later!

PRINCESS: Of course, some of us will be widows.

ENID: *You,* dear, for one.

PRINCESS [*with a sigh*]: Looking back, how droll it seems.

ENID [*diffident, cautious*]: Looking back at what?

PRINCESS: At everything.

ENID: This mystic side to you, Zena, is it something new?

PRINCESS: No.

ENID: Your late husband—did he know of it?

PRINCESS [*lifting her shoulders slightly*]: He may have guessed.

ENID: Only "guessed."

PRINCESS: Racing, pigeon-shooting, billiards and whist were his chief pleasures.

ENID: An egoist?

PRINCESS [*softly reminiscent*]: Nils was different. He knew . . .

ENID: Who was Nils?

PRINCESS: He was my first.

ENID: Oh?

PRINCESS: I adored him. We *adored* each other. [*With a sigh:*] He was the dearest of *all* my husbands.

ENID: Tell me about him.

PRINCESS: He was not strong. He required always enormous precautions.

ENID: I presume you nursed him.

PRINCESS [*whimsically*]: Such a strange, bored and beautiful face he had . . . though harrowingly thin he was. [*Laughing:*] I sometimes miss his clever imitations of farmyard noises.

ENID [*fascinated*]: Yes?

PRINCESS [*mirthlessly*]: Hee-haw—Cook-a-doodle-doo.

ENID: He must leave a blank. . . .

PRINCESS: I remember he died just as the clock was striking midday. . . .

ENID [*speechless*]: . . . !

PRINCESS [*poignant-eyed*]: Such a charming, such a brilliant man. . . . He begged me to mourn him in Chinese fashion—White.

ENID: Which, of course, you did?

PRINCESS: And then, when all the wreaths were spread [*demonstrating*], I danced a *gavotte* over his grave.

ENID: He was not the explorer?

PRINCESS: Oh no.

ENID: What was *he* like?

PRINCESS [*evasively*]: Poor Phil—I forget what it was I didn't like about him. . . .

ENID [*prompt*]: His beard.

PRINCESS: Phil had no beard.

ENID: Which was the one that had?

PRINCESS: Hugh. He broke my heart.

ENID [*after an instant*]: Oh, isn't God far off? Zena! Isn't He, dear?

PRINCESS [*unruffled, abbessish*]: No, Enid. I don't think He is—not very.

ENID: Don't you?

PRINCESS [*smiling*]: Certainly I don't.

ENID [*impulsive*]: Do you care to understand me better? [*Leaning against* PRINCESS:] Well—I prefer *St John of the Cross* to *St Vincent de Paul!*

PRINCESS: So do I!

ENID [*a slight pause; count "six"*]: I feel I don't want love exactly—but some thrilling friendship. . . .

PRINCESS [*arch, gay, diagnosing*]: You want God, dear.

ENID: God?

PRINCESS: That is what is lacking.

ENID [*as* NADINE *appears*]: If it only were that!

SCENE VI

Same. NADINE

NADINE: I found Angelo in the loggia licking the ices.

ENID: Oh, Nadine.

PRINCESS: Do you go to Doney or Giacosa?

NADINE: Giacosa.

ENID [*moving towards house*]: Oughtn't one to be going in?

NADINE [*following her*]: I suppose one should!

PRINCESS [*dawdling*]: Delightful, the early Dahlias.

NADINE [*to* PRINCESS]: Coming?

[*Exeunt* ENID *and* NADINE *to house. Re-enter* NURSE *from the right bearing little* CHARLES.]

SCENE VII

PRINCESS, NURSE, INFANT

PRINCESS [*observing their names, admiring the dahlias*]: Louis-Philippe, Mrs Marvel—voluptuous Mrs Marvel! [*Bending:*] Principessa Valentine di Odescalchi—a new variety, is it?

NURSE: It's been a glorious day, your Highness, for your godson's christening!

PRINCESS: You made me jump!

NURSE [*holding up infant*]: He's a fine vigorous boy, marm!

PRINCESS: Very.

NURSE: Oh, he's such a lusty little devil!

PRINCESS: He's handsome enough!

NURSE [*tossing him*]: Oh, he's a little sly one.

PRINCESS [*shaking her muff at him*]: He never cried once as he was sprinkled!

NURSE: He never noticed. All the while he was being baptised he was making Turk's eyes at a couple of pig-tails.

PRINCESS: Such a crowd at Santa Maria I've seldom seen.

NURSE: Poor Mrs Sheil-Meyer. People are so sorry for her.

PRINCESS: It's terrible, I know.

NURSE [*voluble, familiar*]: Begging your pardon, marm, but do you think the Master's really dead?

PRINCESS [*surprised*]: I'm much afraid so!

NURSE: I don't, then!

PRINCESS [*arrested*]: Ah?

NURSE: I'm just suspicious. [*Wisely:*] The service I've seen . . .

PRINCESS [*vaguely*]: Well, all the papers . . .

NURSE [*contemptuously*]: The papers!

PRINCESS: And the enquiries that were made . . .

NURSE: I shouldn't wonder, now, if he's not in America.

PRINCESS: In America?

NURSE: He and his friend.

PRINCESS: What makes you think that?

NURSE [*beaming*]: Gracious powers! [*Darkly:*] I've seen what I've seen!

PRINCESS [*raising a drooping dahlia upon its stick*]: Life?

NURSE: It's not for nothing I've gone about as I have!

PRINCESS: And you've no wish at all to settle down?

NURSE: It's all one to me!

PRINCESS [*tentatively*]: I seek a porteress for a house of piety!

NURSE: That wouldn't suit me!

PRINCESS [*reassuring*]: It's an easy enough position.

NURSE: A porter's place in a Sisterhood? [*Dryly:*] You call it settling down?

PRINCESS: Think it over!

NURSE: Let all have their latch-keys, and maybe I will.

SCENE VIII

Same. REGGIE (*hatless, from house*)

REGGIE: I want to hide.

PRINCESS: Hide?

REGGIE: I hadn't thought it possible [*breathlessly*] to meet so many wicked people at a Nursery Tea.

PRINCESS: Who have you run away from?

REGGIE: A withered lily woman.

PRINCESS: There are so many withered lily women [*vaguely*]. Here in Florence.

REGGIE [*saluting* CHARLES]: Please, might I hold him, Nurse?

NURSE: Certainly, sir!

REGGIE [*taking* CHARLES, *considering him*]: He's such a profound-looking baby.

PRINCESS [*dreamily*]: He has *an Ocean* of sleep upon him. . . .

NURSE: Oh, he's a little rascal!

REGGIE [*to* PRINCESS]: I'm told you called me disreputable the other night!

PRINCESS: I'm sure I hardly recollect whether I called you reputable or disreputable—I don't remember.

REGGIE: Unkind.

PRINCESS [*motherly*]: And how are our actual prospects?

REGGIE [*candid*]: If I'm a little disappointed at present I believe always in my own eventual star.

PRINCESS: That's right!

REGGIE: I'm hoping to be a Cardinal's secretary soon.

PRINCESS: *Are* you?

REGGIE: Nothing's quite decided—but I think I've got the job.

PRINCESS: You'll get awfully bored, shan't you, going to conversaziones in the religious world?

REGGIE [*resigned*]: *Forse!*

PRINCESS: Until you assume your duties, I presume you'll remain in Florence?

REGGIE [*returning infant to* NURSE, *who parades slowly with it up and down*]: Lord Orkish has asked me to make his house temporarily my home.

PRINCESS [*after an instant*]: Is *Lady* Orkish coming out this year?

REGGIE: She's been.

PRINCESS: Been?

REGGIE: She only broke her journey on her way from Rome.

PRINCESS [*looking down while she speaks*]: She didn't stay long.

REGGIE: Long enough!

PRINCESS: For Lord Orkish?

REGGIE [*with feeling*]: It made my flesh *creep* to see him in the white custody of a wife.

PRINCESS [*with brio*]: S-s-s-sh! For shame!

REGGIE: I admire the Old Bean! He wears his degradation brilliantly, as though it were *an Order!*

PRINCESS: He talked across me at dinner once and I've not forgiven him for it!

REGGIE: It's awful, I know, when he begins about "The Cabal that rose up against me!"

PRINCESS: Oh, I'm terrified of him then!

REGGIE [*perceiving* LORD ORKISH]: And, it appears, here we have him.

[*Enter* LORD ORKISH.]

SCENE IX

Same. LORD ORKISH

LORD ORKISH: I've come as an emissary to say that tea is being served in the house.

PRINCESS: I don't want tea, thanks.

LORD ORKISH: Perhaps you'd care for an ice?

PRINCESS [*emphatic*]: No.

REGGIE: Why do you say "No" in such a voice?

PRINCESS: Never mind.

LORD ORKISH: Lady Wilson-Philipson has just arrived with an octet of daughters like cabbage-roses—so large, so pink, so fresh.

[*Violins sound faintly from house.*]

REGGIE: It's going to be a crush!

PRINCESS: I think I'll go in, as Monsignor Vanhove may perhaps be in the drawing room.

[*Exit* PRINCESS *to house.*]

SCENE X

LORD ORKISH, REGGIE

LORD ORKISH: I missed you in the Piazza.

REGGIE: Mr Hope offered me a lift up in his carriage.

LORD ORKISH [*leering a little*]: I wish people would offer *me* lifts.

REGGIE [*amiable*]: I'd as soon have walked.

LORD ORKISH [*dropping into a seat*]: Seen anything at all of his Eminence?

REGGIE [*emotionally*]: Not half an hour ago—in furs, and a soft tulle hat like an Oxford mist.

LORD ORKISH: You didn't attack him?

REGGIE [*shocked*]: *Me? How could I?*

LORD ORKISH: His pretensions to youth are a little ridiculous.

REGGIE [*seating himself on the ground*]: The first time I went to the Villa —I shall never forget—I think the electric fan just kept me from fainting.

[*Enter* ANGELO, *with a salver and ices.*]

SCENE XI

Same. ANGELO

LORD ORKISH [*refusing ice*]: No, *grazie.*

REGGIE: There is something mediæval to me in his appearance.

LORD ORKISH: Mediæval?

REGGIE [*refusing ice*]: It's his livery.

ANGELO [*smiling*]: The Signora will be sad you do not like her ice.

REGGIE: What are they?

ANGELO: This lemon, this pistachio—

REGGIE: And this?

ANGELO [*languid*]: *Chi lo sa?*

REGGIE [*venturing*]: Shall I regret it?

95

LORD ORKISH [*to* ANGELO, *fixing him*]: Were you ever in Naples?

ANGELO [*languid*]: Yes; oh yes.

LORD ORKISH: I seem to have seen you.

ANGELO [*displaying his teeth, smiling*]: Via Tavolini!

LORD ORKISH: I dare say.

ANGELO: As a boy I vend flowers.

LORD ORKISH: Via Tavolini?

ANGELO: Now and then I would pose.

REGGIE: Pose?

ANGELO [*gazing indolently over his shoulder-knots*]: I'm a model.

LORD ORKISH [*ironic*]: And so at last I behold a model footman!

ANGELO [*sighing*]: *Ah, caro Dio!*

LORD ORKISH: The perfect servant?

ANGELO [*smiling*]: *Per Bacco!*

REGGIE: You prefer this to Naples?

ANGELO: No.

REGGIE: Nicer Naples.

ANGELO: I want to go to America.

LORD ORKISH: Why do you want to go to America?

ANGELO: *Chi lo sa?*

LORD ORKISH: Young rapscallion!

ANGELO [*rolling his eyes*]: New York.

LORD ORKISH: What should you do in New York?

REGGIE: Yes. [*Rapping it out quickly:*] And what were you doing under the Piazza della Signoria Colonnades the other night?

ANGELO: Piazza della Signoria?

REGGIE: In ambuscade.

ANGELO: *Niente.*

REGGIE [*sceptic*]: *Niente?*

ANGELO [*terrorised*]: Ah, Gesù!

[*Exit* ANGELO, *to house.*]

SCENE XII

LORD ORKISH, REGGIE

LORD ORKISH: It's a pity he's lost his master. Adrian would, of course, have trained him!

REGGIE: Where can he be—he and Eric?

LORD ORKISH: Nobody knows. Where the foxes say good-night to each other, I should think.

REGGIE: It must be a little *triste* for Mrs Sheil-Meyer.

LORD ORKISH: She seems perfectly resigned.

[*Four or five small children emerge from house and scatter like butterflies behind the various bushes.*]

REGGIE: Today she is receiving the felicitations of half Florence.

LORD ORKISH: *Davvero.* So many *he's and she's* I never saw!

[*Enter the* MARCHESA PITTI-CONTI, *peering about as if looking for someone.*]

SCENE XIII

Same. MARCHESA PITTI-CONTI

MARCHESA [*calling*]: Dante, Dan-te Silvio Paolao. [*To* LORD ORKISH *and* REGGIE, *whimsically:*] He has left his mother, my little bundle of a boy. . . .

REGGIE: He can't be very far.

MARCHESA: A *bambino,* it seems, has captured his fancy. [*Peeping down among the dahlias*] He is flirting something outrageously with the sweetest blonde.

LORD ORKISH: Yes?

MARCHESA: It is impossible to resist your English children.

LORD ORKISH [*paternal, trying to look less like a wolf*]: Pretty, attractive tots—

97

MARCHESA [*gracious*]: We Italian women, you know, have an inclination
. . . an *inclination particulière* . . . [*a sigh*] for the English type!

LORD ORKISH: Ah, the English type! But not the English climate?

MARCHESA [*pronouncing every syllable crisply, distinctly*]: Oh, come! It
is not so bad as it is painted. . . . I have some charming recollections of your
country . . . of England. [*Sentimentally:*] Salisbury on a summer morning.
. . . De-licious! [*Introspective:*] I remember I was de-lighted—as well—with
Bath. . . .

LORD ORKISH: One can hardly judge Great Britain from Salisbury and
Bath.

REGGIE [*simpering*]: Or even Stonehenge!

MARCHESA: I don't. [*Proudly:*] I have been much further than that. I have
been in Oxford and in Cambridge. [*Beginning to gesticulate:*] And into the
Hebrides even—yes! I have seen the modern Athens! But no! [*With a gri-
mace:*] Also Abbotsford I was at. [*Ecstatic, cultured:*] Sir Valter Scott! [*Rec-
ollecting herself:*] But Salisbury on a summer morning—Salisbury!

[*She drifts away, peering for her son among the dahlias as* ENID *comes
down.*]

SCENE XIV

Same. ENID. *Later, a little boy; then* GLYDA

LORD ORKISH: The Marchesa is raving of the surpassing splendours of
Salisbury.

REGGIE: Salisbury on a summer morning . . .

ENID: I suppose she's homesick. You know she was *née* Smith, and born
in the Close.

LORD ORKISH: I didn't.

REGGIE [*irrepressible*]: She is like a toy-terrier that bit me.

ENID: S-s-s-s-s-sh! Don't *say* such dreadful things.

REGGIE: Exactly.

ENID [*crossing to hammock and lifting up forgotten crystal, which she proceeds with hierarchic care to wipe*]: They have a gorgeous place . . . near Verona . . . The Pitti-Contis . . . which is mortgaged to the last sod.

LORD ORKISH: What, gazing still?

REGGIE: There's a new man now in the town.

ENID: Oh? Really? You must give me his address.

REGGIE: He lives in the last house of a little mysterious street. You would never find the way.

LORD ORKISH: Have you seen anything yourself, Mrs Tresilian?

ENID [*staring straight before her as though she were Cassandra*]: Today I saw a beautiful little giraffe.

LORD ORKISH: Queer.

ENID: Or a goat it may have been.

REGGIE [*yawning*]: I had a morning dream—I saw goats.

ENID [*uninterested. Changing the subject*]: In autumn the garden is as melancholy as any churchyard.

LORD ORKISH: Oh, don't say so!

REGGIE: Now is the time for Vallombrosa.

ENID: The forest must be beautiful now. . . .

[*Enter, from behind a tree, a* CHILD.]

CHILD: Mother! Where is she?

ENID: I don't know, dear. . . . I expect she's in the house.

[*Exit* CHILD.]

LORD ORKISH: Wasn't that Violet's boy?

ENID: Oh no . . . he's four—and has the air of a budding policeman.

[*Enter* GLYDA, très affairée *in a "Botticelli" frock.*]

GLYDA: Aren't you going in for any refreshment?

REGGIE: Thanks. I've already had an ice!

GLYDA [*to* ENID]: The new American actress "Ondelette" has offered to recite.

REGGIE [*bored*]: Oh?

GLYDA [*important*]: *The Prayer of Akhnaton to the Sun.* . . .

LORD ORKISH: She gave it only lately at the Harkovs'.

REGGIE: And I heard her do it at the Villa White [*mimicking*], "Oh, Akhnaton! Akhnaton!"

99

ENID [*shrewdly*]: I think the sunlight has gone to her head.

REGGIE [*taking crystal from* ENID]: Let me see.

ENID: Be careful.

REGGIE [*consulting crystal*]: A nigger! [*Shouts.*]

LORD ORKISH [*leaning over him*]: Only *one?*

[LORD ORKISH *and* REGGIE *appear enthralled.*]

GLYDA: Mamma has had to go to a private exhibition; but she's coming on.

ENID [*vague*]: Of what?

GLYDA [*seating herself*]: Of Pictures.

ENID: Oh.

GLYDA: Portraits . . . all by women. Carriera, Kauffman, Morisot, Le Brun—

ENID: *Fade,* I should think.

GLYDA [*arch*]: It's such fun though in Italy, being a woman!

ENID: Why?

GLYDA: I don't know—but it's such fun!!

ENID: Well, you're only a little girl yet.

GLYDA: You should see the way I'm looked at.

ENID: Where?

GLYDA: Where! Oh, in the street—in church. The other day, in the railway-carriage coming back from Milan—

ENID: Well?

GLYDA [*confused*]: A young officer—oh, how he stared. My goodness!

ENID: The Italians, I find, are very easily impressed.

GLYDA [*ideal*]: Love's a dose of heaven!

ENID: You modern girls are far too cute.

GLYDA [*after a hesitation*]: I cannot resist telling you . . . I've seen him again. . . .

ENID [*vague*]: Who?

GLYDA: The Officer!

ENID: What is this craving after *orange-blossom?* . . . They would persuade us it seems a woman's chief aim is a march to the altar.

GLYDA: He's deliciously dark—a regular raven, my dear.

ENID: What next?

GLYDA [*longingly*]: Beautiful, Tall, and Mysterious Man!

ENID: Oh.

GLYDA [*tenderly*]: It was in the Cascine . . .

ENID: He didn't speak?

GLYDA [*moved*]: No . . . but as he came towards me it was like a *strain* of music.

[*Enter, from house,* NADINE, PRINCESS *and* MONSIGNOR VANHOVE.]

SCENE XV

Same. NADINE, PRINCESS *and* MONSIGNOR VANHOVE. *He is dressed in something subtly chic; he looks a lover of delicatessen.*

MONSIGNOR [*to* NADINE]: Ah! Rome, Rome, in the days of Julia Farnese . . .

NADINE [*distrait*]: I suppose it must have been.

PRINCESS [*to* ENID]: Come here, dear, and be introduced. . . . I want you to know each other.

NADINE [*to* LORD ORKISH *and* REGGIE]: They're dancing the *farandole.* Quick and choose your partner.

LORD ORKISH [*objecting*]: My dancing days are over quite.

NADINE [*taking him and* REGGIE *up stage*]: I'll not believe it!

[*Exeunt* LORD ORKISH *and* REGGIE *to house.*]

[*Re-enter* NURSE *and infant, accompanied by a squadron of small children. She holds a story-book. Crossing to pillared circle, she seats herself sedately below the Virgin with the children grouped about her.* GLYDA *shortly joins them.*]

SCENE XVI

ENID, PRINCESS, MONSIGNOR VANHOVE, *then* NADINE

PRINCESS: And so the Pope lends his authority!

MONSIGNOR [*twirling his thumbs*]: We have his prayers, his wishes.

PRINCESS: His prayers, his wishes!

ENID: What could you want more, dearest?

PRINCESS [*holding out her hand to her—the one with the muff*]: You dear girl—and Nadine!

ENID [*sublime*]: She would never leave her child.

MONSIGNOR [*significantly*]: Whoever doth not take up the cross and follow Me, cannot be My disciple.

PRINCESS [*with feeling*]: My dear Monsignor.

MONSIGNOR: And isn't it so?

PRINCESS [*exalted, audacious*]: I never wanted a child, I think, till now.

ENID [*frivolous, laughing*]: Will you not be such a cynic.

PRINCESS: My dear, I mean it.

ENID [*in an undertone*]: Peculiar devotion . . .

PRINCESS: And what is going on down in Rome?

MONSIGNOR: Few functions . . .

PRINCESS: It's full early yet.

MONSIGNOR [*blinking*]: There was a ball the other evening at the Grand Hotel.

PRINCESS: Oh, whose?

MONSIGNOR: The Longfields'.

PRINCESS: I hear she, Lady Longfield, is working havoc amongst the Cardinals, with her copper hair, large moist eyes and liquid voice.

MONSIGNOR: And she also subscribes to everything.

PRINCESS: It makes one feel so jealous.

MONSIGNOR [*suave*]: You are not forgotten.

PRINCESS: No?

MONSIGNOR: Cardinal Ventifiore very often speaks of you.

PRINCESS: He took me round Trastevere once. It stands out vividly in my mind like *a first infidelity*.

MONSIGNOR: And Dom Jonquil too.

PRINCESS: I remember him, a great jaded-looking boy, almost as pale as the young man in St Mark's who shows one the Pala d'Oro.

ENID [*deliberatingly*]: I suppose, Zena, a long grey tangle of a veil?

PRINCESS: Where?

ENID: I was thinking of our uniforms.

PRINCESS: All that, of course, is in my prospectus.

NADINE [*coming down*]: Monsignor Vanhove! *Is* it true they intend to build a new Embassy? The front *quite* windowless, the back *all* glass?

MONSIGNOR [*blinking*]: It's the first I've heard of it.

NURSE [*serenely reading*]: "Then the wicked witch smeared her little limbs with ram's-grease and twisted her round three times! In a trice, the walls of the humble cottage fell away, and the palace appeared before them."

PRINCESS: Who told you, Nadine, about the Embassy?

NADINE: Mr Hope.

PRINCESS: What should "Tozhy" know?

NADINE [*looking round*]: I'm so nervous of him. Since his exile here he has become a sort of public loofah.

NURSE [*continuing—on the crest of her tale*]: "From that same minute the princess determined to follow the dictates of her heart, and refused to listen any longer to the worldly maxims of the King and Queen."

MONSIGNOR: Ah, sweet innocents!

NADINE [*indicating a child*]: See that little gollywog there? . . . She's the Pontiff's niece.

ENID: Oh?

NADINE: The Pope is her uncle

MONSIGNOR: She will become florid in time, like her mother.

PRINCESS [*glancing towards the tree-tops*]: Hark to the birds! How happy they must be. *Singing, singing, singing.* Nearer to heaven than *we* are!

[*Enter* BLANCHE NEGRESS.]

103

SCENE XVII

Same. BLANCHE. *She is wearing a tailor-made "Redfern" and a man's cravat.*

BLANCHE: I've come to know if I may enrol myself?

PRINCESS: Eh?

BLANCHE: I happened to hear you're starting a Sisterhood—not *too* strait-laced; and I wish to offer myself as a probationer.

PRINCESS: Certainly; if you've any Vocation at all!

BLANCHE: My work is over in the world, you see. I have nothing to fight for now.

PRINCESS: Are you even giving up your pen?

BLANCHE [*confused*]: No . . . but hotels and lodgings *are* such noisy places.

PRINCESS [*doubtfully*]: I see . . .

BLANCHE [*rather wildly*]: Noise! Noise! Noise!

PRINCESS: But are there no quiet rooms, back rooms, in back hotels—and in back places?

BLANCHE [*tragically*]: I hate a silence that isn't *real.*

PRINCESS [*graciously*]: Well, in the cypress-alleys of our Anchorage, I trust you will find inspiration.

[*Enter* LADY ROCKTOWER]

BLANCHE: I'm sure I shall; I feel it.

SCENE XVIII

Same. LADY ROCKTOWER

LADY ROCKTOWER: I was obliged to go to the P. V. of the women-artists.

NADINE [*offering hand*]: I adore Private Views!

LADY ROCKTOWER: This was *so* dull.

PRINCESS: Everybody's here!

LADY ROCKTOWER: Some things are such an index. [*Intensely:*] Violet is parting with her *Rosalba*. . . .

NADINE: I wonder why?

PRINCESS: She's become so mercenary. She seems to have now a sort of *hunger* for money.

ENID: Disgusting!

LADY ROCKTOWER: I fancy she gives it . . .

MONSIGNOR [*alert*]: Ah?

LADY ROCKTOWER [*in an undertone*]: To a tall, dark man in the Pope's body-guard!

BLANCHE [*breathlessly*]: I suppose her lover?

MONSIGNOR: In my opinion, a woman may accept the consolations of Bacchus as soon as accept a lover.

PRINCESS: Do you really think she may?

ENID: Still every now and then one's face needs transforming. And Love does it better than anything else!

MONSIGNOR: It depends, my child, upon the *sort*.

PRINCESS: I suppose when one's husband is fifty-seven . . .

LADY ROCKTOWER: My dear, even a man of fifty-seven is better than nothing at all.

BLANCHE: I don't agree.

LADY ROCKTOWER: No?

BLANCHE: I've been married, you know, too. Yet I sometimes think the simple comfort of a hot-water bottle . . .

PRINCESS [*laughing*]: Well, I'm going to speak to the Wilson-Philipsons! I see Vicky over there.

[*A few persons emerge from house as if to enjoy the scene, which begins to take on the aspect of sunset.*]

BLANCHE: I mean to be off-hand with her. She translates every one into terms of colour, and I hear she called me a dirty white.

NADINE: She's *guapa,* as they say in Spain!

LADY ROCKTOWER: Poor things, they live, no one quite knows how.

ENID: I passed them all the other evening in a covered bullock-cart in the Viale dei Colli.

NADINE: Oh?

ENID: I just *moaned* for joy! The big tears rolling!

[*Re-enter* MARCHESA PITTI-CONTI *with her son* DANTE. *He is sobbing. He has evidently been misbehaving himself. The* MARCHESA *seems furious—her English is perfect.*]

SCENE XIX

Same. Plus MARCHESA *and* DANTE SILVIO PAOLAO

DANTE [*sobbing*]: Boo-oo-oo! Ow-ow-ow!

MARCHESA: Did not your father give you the choice, wicked little boy [*pinching him*], of Oxford, Cambridge, Salamanca, Utrecht, Harvard, Glasgow, Edinburgh or Heidelberg?

DANTE: Boo-oo-oo!

LADY ROCKTOWER [*turning*]: Are you thinking of sending him to school?

MARCHESA: Ah, *chère madame . . .!*

LADY ROCKTOWER: *Il est gentil ce grand gosse.* [*To* ENID:] *Je trouve qu'il est en train de devenir charmant.*

ENID: *N'est-ce pas?*

MARCHESA [*to* BLANCHE]: *Bonjour, chère amie.*

BLANCHE [*all there*]: *Come va?*

MARCHESA: *Bene, grazie; e lei?*

BLANCHE [*all there still*]: *Benissimo!*

LADY ROCKTOWER: To what school—*a che scuola*—shall you send him?

MARCHESA [*very foreign*]: I do not know.

LADY ROCKTOWER: School, in my time, was not the soft place it is today.

MARCHESA: No?

LADY ROCKTOWER: As a young girl I used to be whipped with furze.

MARCHESA [*appalled*]: Ah, *chère madame . . .*

LADY ROCKTOWER [*cheerfully, rearranging the back of her dress*]: I was all gorse-marks often!

[*Re-enter* LORD ORKISH]

106

SCENE XX

Same. Plus LORD ORKISH

LORD ORKISH: Young Astix is in the loggia.

NADINE: Is he?

LORD ORKISH: People are making such a fuss.

NADINE: Absurd. His slender volume of verses, you could pass it under the door. . . .

LORD ORKISH [*with indifference*]: I dare say.

NADINE: Why aren't you dancing?

LORD ORKISH: I'm too old.

NADINE: Or too lazy, which!

MONSIGNOR: At the fall, Florence tends to make one sluggish.

LADY ROCKTOWER: Yes; the autumn here is certainly enervating. Only this very morning I said to Dr Mater, in the Boboli Gardens: "I have that *tired* feeling, Doctor, again," I said; "and I can't think what it can be." "Oh, Lady Rocktower," he said to me, with his piercing glance, "I assure you it's nothing but the change of season."

MONSIGNOR: Exactly.

LADY ROCKTOWER: I'll be glad, though, I confess, for Lord Rocktower's sake, when winter sets in.

LORD ORKISH: And how is my old pal Harry?

LADY ROCKTOWER: We all thought him passing out a day or two ago. Dr Mater told me—but oh, so sweetly, oh, so gently—he could do nothing more, when suddenly he sat up and asked for lobster soup. Lobster soup! There was none in the house, but within an hour the soup was made—and he was saved!

LORD ORKISH: Bravo!

LADY ROCKTOWER: Every time I let the Villa he seems to quite give way. [*With a sigh of resignation:*] Lord Rocktower loves Florence and he loathes leaving it. . . .

LORD ORKISH: I don't wonder.

MARCHESA [*to* DANTE, *who is making grimaces at the Pope's niece*]:

Macché, macché!

ENID [*to* DANTE]: Come, and I will gather you a few dahlias.

[*She takes* MARCHESA *and* DANTE *up stage towards a flower-plat, while* NADINE *and* MONSIGNOR *cross to pillared circle where* NURSE *is seated.* BLANCHE *during progress of scene has joined the little group which is watching sunset.*]

LORD ORKISH: I suppose, if Mrs Sheil-Meyer withdraws from Society, the *next* villa to let will be this!

LADY ROCKTOWER: I've no patience at all with her if she does.

LORD ORKISH: The Princess Zoubaroff can be very persuasive.

LADY ROCKTOWER [*with rigour*]: It's all very fine for Zena, who is no longer in her Springtime, to retire. Six husbands must have left her with the minimum of a heart! But for a young and pretty woman like Nadine Sheil-Meyer to give up the world, it's another matter.

LORD ORKISH: Mrs Tresilian is sure to follow suit!

LADY ROCKTOWER: *Que de sottises!*

LORD ORKISH: From sympathy.

LADY ROCKTOWER: She trifles—she truffles—but I can't think she will.

LORD ORKISH [*sententious*]: The Princess is one of those who, when they cast their spell—

LADY ROCKTOWER: I always stick up for Zena Zoubaroff. I don't believe *half* I hear about her! Although I dare say a *good deal* is true!

[*They both laugh.*]

LORD ORKISH: It's a pity their husbands can't appear just to bring them to their bearing.

[*The* farandole *is heard.*]

LADY ROCKTOWER: Oh, they're coming out!

SCENE XXI

General

Children, hand in hand, emerge from house. Making a ring, they proceed to dance about the garden Temple.

LORD ORKISH: Youth, youth.

PRINCESS [*approaching*]: I feel I want to dance!

LADY ROCKTOWER: My dear Zena!

PRINCESS: I've had Austrian Waltzes whirling through my head all day.

[REGGIE *is seen in the background pirouetting with* MR ASTIX, *the author —a wild young man who looks like the Publishers' Ruin.*]

LADY ROCKTOWER: Oh . . . look at Reggie.

LORD ORKISH [*moved*]: Dear, dear boy.

MONSIGNOR [*coming forward, benign*]: Everywhere delicious inno-cence!

PRINCESS [*boxing, con amore, with her muff each little girl upon the ears as she goes by*]: Nun! Nun! Nun!

THE CURTAIN FALLS

ACT III

Same scene. A few of the trees have shed their leaves. It is Winter. Through the bare branches of the Judas-trees a Calvary is visible at the extremity of the garden.

As the curtain rises, NURSE *is seen strolling to and fro, exercising baby in his pram.*

ANGELO *follows at her heels, singing strenuously to the guitar.*

NURSE *and* INFANT, ANGELO

NURSE: You young Italians are all passion.

ANGELO [*rhapsodically, carolling*]: Tra-li-lal-la!

NURSE: Not so loud, you'll wake the child. [*She takes from the pram a flask of Lacrima Christi and drinks.*]

ANGELO: *Sapristi?*

NURSE: My favourite vintage! Plenty of body . . .

ANGELO: *Ah, che roba!*

NURSE: Yes, you Italians are dangerous fellows. . . .[*Sentimentally:*] You make me think of Dudley, Lord Bellforest's under-butler, long ago. [*Drinks.*] Ah, I've been a buxom woman in my day, dear. . . . A little bit of proper *simpatico* I was! And I'm good-enough yet, honey. . . . Some constitutions are just like this [*drinking*], they improve with time. [*Falling into reflection:*] She was forty-nine years old when she had me—my dear mother. And then there were two after that.

110

ANGELO [*shrugging*]: *Che volete?*

NURSE [*cogent*]: Which is more than most of them could say (or do), your Tuscan Signoras!

ANGELO [*indignant*]: I am not Tuscan myself at all. [*Strumming his guitar.*] My home is in the South. Ah *bella* Taormina!

NURSE [*sentimentally*]: Well; it's all South to me, dear.

ANGELO [*shrugging*]: *Per Bacco.*

NURSE: This is South all right for me [*returning flask to pram*].

ANGELO [*yawning*]: How dull it is—*ah, Dio.*

NURSE: It's quiet enough, it's true, now the mistress has gone.

ANGELO: *Povera!*

NURSE: I like a place, I must say, where there's a bit of life. When I was with the Hon. Mrs Cortez, there was company if you like! Valets, chauffeurs, Parisian maids . . . gracious powers, you could take your choice. It was in her establishment [*sighs*] I met my Albert.

ANGELO: Albert?

NURSE: Mr Mangrove—my *sposo!*

[*She sighs several times heavily.*]

ANGELO [*with morbid interest*]: And was he *tutto . . . tutto . . .?*

NURSE [*nodding*]: *Tutto, tutto!* That is to say, my dear, I never could bear him but in the one capacity. . . . For, he never had any mind; or any understanding. . . . What was he [*snaps her fingers*] but that!!

ANGELO: Ah!

NURSE [*archly winking*]: But in the one capacity of love he was unexcelled.

[*Baby begins to require attention.*]

[*Enter* REGGIE *from roadway.*]

SCENE II

Same. REGGIE

REGGIE [*dapper, smiling*]: I blew in only to say good-morning to little Charles.

NURSE: That's very kind of you, sir. [*Raising baby:*] Sit up and say good-morning to Mr Quintus!

REGGIE: He's a fine child, Nurse.

NURSE: He's a little beauty, sir, as I'm his sainted nanny! [*Confidential:*] They won't have him inside the convent, heaven protect us, for fear he'd flurry the nuns!

REGGIE: Will you kiss me, Charles?

NURSE: Kiss the gentleman. . . .

REGGIE: That's right.

NURSE: See how he's laughing.

REGGIE: The rogue! I fear he's a rogue, Nurse.

NURSE: He's a fine fellow.

REGGIE: No morals!!! He has no morals, I fear. . . .

NURSE: Oh! Why, sir, why now?

REGGIE: Born in Florence, a boy very rarely has.

NURSE: Don't be hard on Florence, Mr Quintus, it's not near so fast, I'm sure, as San Francisco.

REGGIE: I wonder?

ANGELO [*wistfully*]: Ah, America . . .

REGGIE: Still keen as ever on visiting the States?

ANGELO [*with all the languor of "the South"*]: Yes; oh yes.

REGGIE [*twinkling mysteriously*]: Before you go, I must give you a letter of introduction to a multi-millionaire—who's rather a friend of mine!—in Memphis, Tennessee.

ANGELO [*delighted*]: *Tante grazie!*

REGGIE: *Niente.*

[*The bell tinkles. Murmuring his gratitude,* ANGELO *answers the garden-gate, after which he exits to house.*]

[*Enter, from roadway,* BLANCHE.]

SCENE III

Same. BLANCHE. *She looks hot and dishevelled. She bears a sack. She is dressed as a Nun. She gives one the impression rather of an escaped peacock.*

BLANCHE [*dropping her sack*]: They sent me to wait here, with the victuals. [*Groaning:*] Out at Monte Serravizza there isn't a thing.

REGGIE: What? Are they coming up to the Villa today?

BLANCHE: Yes.

[NURSE, *on hearing this intelligence, briefly withdraws.*]

REGGIE: The whole cortège?

BLANCHE [*seating herself, mopping her brow*]: We came into Florence—shopping, or begging—God knows which . . .

REGGIE [*amused*]: A bit of both, I expect.

BLANCHE: My wretched nerves; has Baccio Bertucci been?

REGGIE: Baccio Bertucci?

BLANCHE: He promised.

REGGIE [*mystified*]: What?

BLANCHE [*occult*]: It can't be helped. I suppose we must go without.

REGGIE: Your Abbess, I'm told, is quite scoring as a Saint.

BLANCHE [*irritated*]: Tsch! Who said so?

REGGIE: The Rocktowers.

BLANCHE [*intensely*]: Life at Monte Serravizza is quite indescribable.

REGGIE: It must be wonderful.

BLANCHE: It's nothing but backbiting from morning to night.

REGGIE: Oh!

BLANCHE: The violence of religious jealousy, I know of nothing at all that can match it.

REGGIE: Violence?

BLANCHE: Zena's becoming much too tyrannical.

113

REGGIE [*perching himself on a garden-chair*]: Remember, these small sub-lunar trials will one day pass!

BLANCHE: I hope so, I'm sure.

REGGIE: Poor Mrs Negress.

BLANCHE: Today—as we were coming into Florence—I arranged my side hair [*simpering*] experimentally, and she was *furious.* What are you doing with *those whiskers?* she said to me. I won't have any whiskers here, arousing our thoughts. . . .

REGGIE: Oh. . . .

BLANCHE: While her head was scrubbed but yesterday with henna.

REGGIE: She was shampooed you say with henna!

BLANCHE [*stalking up and down, swaying her skirts from side to side like a Spanish dancer*]: And only the day before she ordered herself a crystal cincture from Paris.

REGGIE [*tossing his hat*]: Olé, olé.

BLANCHE: Thoughts indeed!

REGGIE [*admiringly*]: Nobody can do outrageous things so naturally as she can!

BLANCHE: I admit she's clever. She hushed up the affair of May Winterbottom most successfully.

REGGIE [*awed*]: There's been a scandal?

BLANCHE: A scandal!! The very night the first new novice arrived—

REGGIE: Well?

BLANCHE: Zena smelt smoke. Heavy smoke. All the corridors full of it, coming from the sister's cell. She went to her door and oh the horror.

REGGIE [*breathless*]: What?

BLANCHE: May Winterbottom was smoking Opium.

REGGIE: Pouf!

BLANCHE: Yes.

REGGIE [*rising carelessly*]: If the Princess should want a Pinturicchio for her chapel, by the way, I know where there's one to be found.

BLANCHE: Indeed.

REGGIE: A *Iokanaan.*

BLANCHE: Oh!

REGGIE: Or, I know of a topping Tintoret.

BLANCHE: Thanks . . . but I fancy she's on the scent of a *Sainte Famille* herself.

REGGIE: I'd give a good deal for a permit of inspection!

BLANCHE [*abysmal*]: There's no bathroom yet in the convent . . . you just get caught in the rain. . . .

REGGIE: Disgusting!

BLANCHE [*with a battered smile*]: One of the few drawbacks.

REGGIE [*looking at his watch*]: Well, I must go. I have to meet Lord Orkish in the town.

[*Exit* REGGIE *through garden-gate. Re-enter, at same moment,* NURSE *from house.*]

NURSE: Perhaps you'd prefer, m'm, to rest inside?

BLANCHE: I'm quite happy here.

NURSE: You don't look so, m'm.

BLANCHE: No?

NURSE [*brightly*]: The Religious Life, it's not for everybody!

BLANCHE: No.

NURSE [*confidential*]: She tried to coax me into it. . . . But I didn't feel the call.

BLANCHE: My work was over in the world, you see. I had nothing to fight for. [*To* ENID, *who enters:*] I thought you were *never* coming.

SCENE IV

Enter from roadway ENID, *followed by* NADINE *and* PRINCESS. NADINE *runs to baby's pram.* PRINCESS (*she holds a tortoise-shell cat, like an unhappy "Society" woman, in her arms*) *hovers a moment speaking to someone outside the gate. They look very pale, slim and Isis-like in their grain-coloured Nuns' toilettes.*

ENID [*coming down*]: Sorry to be late, old girl.

BLANCHE [*mortified*]: Old girl . . .

ENID: We've been getting ribbons from Monte—such a subtle old flow-ered-velvet, and yards and yards and *yards* of green Georgette . . .

BLANCHE [*aggrieved, staring at her sack*]: What for?

ENID [*airily*]: Decoration.

PRINCESS [*in great good-humour*]: Today, as a special treat, we're going back by auto!

BLANCHE: Hallelujah!

PRINCESS: Did you do all my little commissions?

BLANCHE: All except the candles.

PRINCESS: Tiresome.

ENID: You look hot.

BLANCHE: My face must be a looking-glass.

PRINCESS: Not that.

BLANCHE: Had that dreadful sack weighed much more I think I should have fainted.

PRINCESS [*a little guilty, excusing herself*]: My dear, I'm desolate you should have had to carry it at all about the streets, but what *could* I do?

BLANCHE [*containing herself*]: Reggie Quintus has just gone.

PRINCESS: Really? And I had wanted to see him.

BLANCHE: He was telling me of a Tintoret, or something.

ENID [*nodding*]: He's rather a judge.

NADINE [*leaning over pram, sorrowfully, to her son*]: My poor pigeon . . . I warn you to expect nothing very much from life.

PRINCESS: What makes her so oppressed?

ENID: She's chagrined a little because I said her habit made her look hunched.

BLANCHE [*critically*]: Distorted. And so it does!

ENID: And she was dreaming again of Adrian.

PRINCESS: Once I get a decent cook she'll not have these nightmares.

[BLANCHE *draws away a little, joining* NADINE.]

ENID: I'm so glad I'm not haunted with Eric!

PRINCESS [*angelic, virtuous*]: May white dreams attend you always, dear. Amen.

ENID [*earnestly*]: Amen.

PRINCESS [*catching marvellously her breath, as if her spirit, freed, had shot from earth to heaven, and from heaven (back again) to earth*]: Ah!

ENID: Blanche seems nervy today.

PRINCESS [*fluttered, breathless yet*]: Yes; unstrung. . . .

ENID: She says she feels "jumpy."

PRINCESS [*with sudden brusqueness*]: Can you wonder her nerves are what they are when she's sipping alternative coffee and tea from seven in the morning to twelve at night?

[*Enter from house,* LADY ROCKTOWER.]

SCENE V

Same. LADY ROCKTOWER. *She looks slightly embarrassed: her face is a trifle red. She is wearing the family pearls. She has a hole in her veil.*

LADY ROCKTOWER: I saw you go by and guessed you'd be here.

[ENID *retreats.*]

PRINCESS [*kissing her* à la Sainte Thérèse]: My dear Lady Rocktower?

LADY ROCKTOWER [*clutching her pearls*]: I've come only to know if, dear —by *any* chance—you could take my daughter in.

PRINCESS [*stiffening*]: Take her in?

LADY ROCKTOWER: Receive her.

PRINCESS: As a novice?

LADY ROCKTOWER: For a time.

PRINCESS [*uncomfortable, suspicious*]: I fear she'd not be happy at Monte Serravizza; I fear our austerities—our Rule—everything!

LADY ROCKTOWER [*candid, frank*]: Glyda's so difficult and so giddy, and it's precisely for that.

PRINCESS [*ethereal, exquisite*]: I was once heedless too!

LADY ROCKTOWER: I would like to marry my daughter straight from your Convent door.

PRINCESS [*still evasive*]: Marry her?

LADY ROCKTOWER [*with much dignity*]: Well—*un grand mariage!*

PRINCESS [*reassured a little*]: But . . . could one manage her?

LADY ROCKTOWER: I am sure you could. And oh [*her voice breaks*], I should be so grateful.

PRINCESS: From what you say, I gather she's given her heart to someone.

LADY ROCKTOWER [*making a clean breast of it*]: Poor child, she thinks herself in love with a young Italian lieutenant . . . though I thank God on my knees, dear Zena, she has scarcely caught a glimpse of his shadow . . . !

PRINCESS: You're certain of that?

LADY ROCKTOWER: Positive.

PRINCESS: I'll come over one morning and have a quiet chat with Glyda—she and I, quite cosy! [*Laughing a little.*] Although, really, I'm most awfully busy at present with my liqueur.

LADY ROCKTOWER: What liqueur?

PRINCESS: I'm inventing a delightfully potent liqueur to be made by the nuns. The Holy Father [*rippling*] was quite charmed with the few distilled drops I sent. He pretends . . . he pretends it will inspire him for Life!

LADY ROCKTOWER: Yes?

PRINCESS: We mean to call it Yellow-Ruin. . . .

LADY ROCKTOWER: I had an audience—my fifth!—only the other day.

PRINCESS: My dear, you're always trotting to Rome!

LADY ROCKTOWER: I adore it in Winter.

PRINCESS: Is there lots and lots going on?

LADY ROCKTOWER: The usual thing, there's been a function at the Quirinal which was dull, and another at the Embassy, which was worse . . . and *apropos* of recent Diplomacy, Lady Winifred Wheeler has just presented Sir Walter Wheeler with a black child. Such a commotion as there's been over it all.

PRINCESS [*horror-struck*]: Black?

LADY ROCKTOWER: Well, dear, dark; but, *oh,* so dark!

PRINCESS [*laughing*]: And the du Wilsons are just starting a Nursery, too.

LADY ROCKTOWER: Poor little Violet . . . ! She made me such a wan, sensitive smile in the street just now.

PRINCESS: She seems to think she should be asked to paint herself for the Uffizi. [*Hilarious:*] Really, I never saw such cheeks!

LADY ROCKTOWER: No; nor I. [*Laughing, going.*] Look in Thursday at the

Villa, if you're able. [*Persuasively:*] Sonino is singing . . .

PRINCESS: Sonino? Oh, when Sonino sings, one visualises everything one wishes!

LADY ROCKTOWER: She is to throw in her sob of love, and sing three solos, for a special charge.

PRINCESS: It's hard indeed to refuse, but we *never* go out at night. . . .

LADY ROCKTOWER: This once! Oh, and I nearly forgot, I wanted to ask you for that choice receipt. Cocks' combs . . . ?

PRINCESS: And the hearts of artichokes!

LADY ROCKTOWER [*smiling, committing it to memory*]: *And the hearts of artichokes!*

PRINCESS [*impressively*]: Crush well.

LADY ROCKTOWER: A more delicious dish . . . you must give it me when I come to you—the days I visit Glyda.

PRINCESS [*leaning on* LADY ROCKTOWER's *arm, and accompanying her towards the gate*]: I'm allowing the novices on feast days to receive their friends in a charming cognac chiffon.

LADY ROCKTOWER: You all look so interesting, as it is!

PRINCESS [*very much pleased*]: Do we?

LADY ROCKTOWER: I almost envy you. . . .

PRINCESS: Dear Lady Rocktower, perhaps some day—

LADY ROCKTOWER [*as she goes out*]: Who knows? A husband's often a strain, and mine's not a world-loving nature very.

SCENE VI

Same. Minus LADY ROCKTOWER

NADINE [*advancing—during* LADY ROCKTOWER's *visit she has withdrawn from view behind a tree*]: And how has he kept, Nurse, all the week?

NURSE: Well as could be, thank you, marm.

NADINE: Poor spirit—!

NURSE: Oh, he's a little rascal!

Ronald Firbank

NADINE: His little laugh does one good.

ENID [*quizzingly*]: He's a remarkably hideous child. Like a remarkably hideous duck . . .

PRINCESS [*abbessish*]: Prioress! Prioress!

ENID [*dancing mischievously about the pram*]: Who ever had such a wobbly chin? Or such a nervous, uncertain nose?

NADINE: He's like his father!

ENID: Ugly . . . ugly . . . like papa.

NURSE [*crooningly*]: *Where's Daddy???*

[*Enter, from garden-gate,* ADRIAN *and* ERIC. *They both are looking wonderfully recouped and rejuvenated—as though their extensive holiday had done them good. Which has benefited from his freedom most—which looks the handsomer—it is not easy to determine.*]

NADINE: When he starts pummelling the air with his little pinkie-winkie fists, with his little dimpled doigts, whatever can it be? I know he wants something. . . .

ADRIAN: Probably *his Father!*

[*Slow music: A short Intermezzo (of a particularly "cloying" nature), coming from the Orchestra, concludes the scene.*]

SCENE VII

Same. ADRIAN, ERIC

NADINE [*the Intermezzo ended, very calmly through the hood of the pram*]: Oh, Adrian, so you have come back!

ADRIAN: As you see.

ENID [*to* ERIC]: You might have given us a sign.

ERIC [*shortly*]: 'Drian's been ill—we were unwilling to alarm you.

ENID [*with biting satire*]: Alarm us!

ADRIAN: Do you remember how scared you were in Egypt once?

NADINE: I can't say I do.

ADRIAN: There's no use to cut up rough.

120

NADINE [*trenchantly*]: You're unwanted.

ENID: Quite unwanted!

PRINCESS [*interposing*]: Your wives are Dedicated!

ADRIAN: I beg your pardon?

ENID [*to* NADINE]: Don't they jar.

ERIC [*catching her by the veil*]: Lor' lummie, what's this?

ENID [*furious*]: Don't touch me!

ERIC [*assertive*]: That's as *I* choose.

ENID [*freeing herself*]: Oh, the horrid man—he hit me.

PRINCESS: He *hit* you?

BLANCHE [*wailing*]: Sacrilege!

ENID [*smacking* ERIC *smartly with her rosary*]: Ah! Monster!

NURSE [*panting*]: Well, I never.

[ANGELO *appears.*]

NADINE [*crucified*]: S-s-s-sh! Avoid a *scena* before the servants.

ERIC: Aie. . . .

BLANCHE [*hysterically*]: Oh! This is awful.

ANGELO [*announcing*]: The auto . . .

ENID [*quietly, threatening him with her scourge*]: Oh, Eric . . . don't exasperate me more!

NADINE [*with the upturned glance of a martyr*]: I refuse to wrangle.

PRINCESS [*inviolate, evoking Calvary*]: Come!

ENID [*doing a little picturesque skirmishing*]: Beast!

ERIC: The bitch bit me.

BLANCHE [*picking up her sack and making for the gate*]: My knees refuse to carry me.

NADINE: Yes. Let's go.

ADRIAN [*indifferent*]: As you please!

NURSE [*to* NADINE]: *I wish to give warning!*

NADINE [*callous*]: Very well.

PRINCESS [*to* NADINE *and* ENID]: Come, chicks!

NADINE [*in her vividest voice*]: Mind the *step*, Zena.

PRINCESS [*turning defiantly at gate*]: The Vatican shall hear of this!

[*Exeunt* PRINCESS, NADINE *and* ENID.]

121

SCENE VIII

ADRIAN, ERIC

ADRIAN [*dropping into a chair*]: I thought perhaps we should find they'd remarried or something, but I'll be cursed if I thought they'd console themselves as they have!

ERIC [*at pram*]: The boy must be yours?

ADRIAN [*blushing, confused*]: I *suppose* I'm his father . . .

ERIC: What on earth are you going to do with the little beggar?

ADRIAN: I shall look out for a school for him tomorrow.

ERIC: No, really, Adrian?

ADRIAN [*loftily*]: I shall set at once about his education.

ERIC [*bending over pram*]: Isn't he just too fat for anything!

[*The outside bell is heard to ring.*]

ADRIAN: What's that?

ERIC [*uneasily*]: My God, if they should have returned. . . .

[*Re-enter* ANGELO. *He saunters languidly over to garden-door.*]

[*Voice of* LORD ORKISH, *off*]: I must have missed Mr Quintus: and I know he comes here most days to play with the child.

[*Voice of* ANGELO, *off*]: The Master has come home!

LORD ORKISH [*entering*]: What?

SCENE IX

Same. LORD ORKISH

ADRIAN [*surprised*]: Henry . . . !

LORD ORKISH [*considerably moved, proffering his hand*]: My dear, dear fellow.

ERIC: Henry?

[*Under the peculiar circumstances, they very nearly all embrace.*]

LORD ORKISH [*wonder-struck*]: And how amazingly fit you look: you seem to have grown much younger.

ERIC [*smiling*]: We've had a top-hole time! 'Drian was seedy, though, at first.

ADRIAN: Nothing at all to speak of!

ERIC: I *refused* to let him die.

ADRIAN [*nodding*]: Eric soon nursed me round!

LORD ORKISH: And your estimable wives—you've heard of them, of course.

ADRIAN: Yes, and seen them too—what's more!

ERIC [*hilarious*]: They must have passed you. They went off in a taxi, a snug half-dozen.

LORD ORKISH: What? They've gone? They've left you? . . .

ADRIAN: Apparently.

ERIC: It's all I can do to believe it.

LORD ORKISH [*with feeling*]: Lucky chaps.

ERIC: Delicious to be so dispossessed . . .

LORD ORKISH [*leering a little*]: Well, they're not the first to come to Florence to turn themselves into prudes!

ADRIAN [*pointedly*]: As *you* very well know, dear Harry.

LORD ORKISH: I take it you'll live apart, as we do—Lady Orkish and I—by "mutual consent."

ERIC: Yes. "Mutual consent."

LORD ORKISH: No odious fuss.

ERIC: I hope not.

LORD ORKISH: I assure you, after the first day I never missed Bella.

ERIC [*stretching luxuriously his arms*]: To be free, to be single!!!

ADRIAN [*addressing rapturously the garden*]: Dear lawn. My own beautiful trees.

LORD ORKISH: He's enchanted to be home. [*Sighing:*] Well, there's no spot on earth to compare with Florence!

[*The outside bell is heard to ring again.* ANGELO *answers it as before. Enter a tiny boy in buttons. He has with him a faggot of huge Church candles.*]

SCENE X

Same. ANGELO, BOY

ANGELO [*having ascertained the boy's business. To* ADRIAN]: He comes from the Church-furnishers in Borgo Santi Apostoli.

ADRIAN: From where?

ANGELO: From Baccio Bertucci's. . . .

ADRIAN [*sharply, to boy*]: Be off with you.

ANGELO: He say the Signora order the candles!

ADRIAN: Tell him to hook it.

ANGELO [*clapping his hands*]: A Monte Serravizza—*laggiù.*

ERIC [*pointing, in desperation*]: *Laggiù, laggiù.*

ANGELO: *Via, via.*

LORD ORKISH [*patting the child's head*]: Run away, there's a good little sinner.

[*Exit boy, followed by* ANGELO.]

SCENE XI

LORD ORKISH, ERIC, ADRIAN, INFANT, *then* ANGELO

ADRIAN: The Eleusinian priestesses weren't in it!

LORD ORKISH: Have you formed yet any plans?

ADRIAN: I shall stop here. It will amuse me infinitely to see what they'll do!

LORD ORKISH [*flippantly*]: I shouldn't wonder much if they weren't back in Lewis hats and diamonds before tonight.

ERIC [*terrified at the idea*]: Oh don't . . . if Enid puts in an appearance again I shall take the first express to Rome.

ADRIAN: You're safe enough, Eric; *Enid has no ties.*

ERIC: No ties?

ADRIAN [*with a touch of conceit*]: She isn't a mother!

LORD ORKISH: It must take an exceptionally "good" woman to forsake husband, son, friends, society, to follow the Way of the Cross.

ADRIAN: It's quite on the cards that Nadine was only bored. Besides, she hasn't deserted her *friends* at all. I believe but for Princess Zoubaroff she'd be here now.

ERIC: The Princess seems to have fairly bewitched them!

LORD ORKISH [*humming pensively to himself*]: With a hey-ho-hey, and a nonny.

ADRIAN: You're right.

LORD ORKISH: I wish she'd rake in Bella.

ADRIAN: Perhaps she will.

LORD ORKISH: And the old white cat . . .

ADRIAN: What old white cat?

LORD ORKISH: The Countess Willie!

[*The baby begins to fidget.*]

ADRIAN [*wheeling the pram about*]: S-s-sh . . . maddening.

LORD ORKISH: I'd like to know what you'll do with him.

ADRIAN: Tomorrow he goes to school.

LORD ORKISH: Does he? By George! Well, I always believe in a boy getting used to the world as soon as possible.

ADRIAN: To be duly prepared.

LORD ORKISH: I know of an incomparable little *Lycée* here in Florence. . . . [*Sighing blissfully.*] Incomparable instructors: incomparable boys. Incomparable, incomparable. Everything incomparable.

ADRIAN [*rather doubtfully*]: I dare say.

LORD ORKISH: Just the thing.

ERIC: Whereabouts is it, Harry?

LORD ORKISH: Via Canta; a vermilion-gold brick Palace in the very heart of the town!

ADRIAN [*bending over pram with smiling raillery*]: We're probably very backward . . . we probably know nothing at all?

[*The baby howls. Re-enter* ANGELO.]

ANGELO: *E' pronto il pranzo!*

ADRIAN [*lightly*]: You'll stay *a pranzo*, Harry?

LORD ORKISH: Thanks.

ADRIAN [*menacingly to baby*]: Stop it!

ERIC: And you shall play us each at pills after, what?

ADRIAN: I hope the nuns haven't injured the cloth!

[*The bell rings violently.*]

ERIC [*paralysed*]: Oh, my God . . . if it should be . . .

[*The garden-gate opens slightly—a handful of leaflets falls inside.*]

LORD ORKISH: *Confetti?*

ADRIAN [*relieved*]: It's only a circular.

ERIC: I thought it was Enid.

LORD ORKISH [*optimistically*]: I wouldn't worry. So long as the Princess chooses, she'll not leave the Sisterhood, I'll be bound.

ERIC: I sincerely hope you're right.

LORD ORKISH [*chuckling to himself*]: And she'll guard her close, believe me!

ERIC [*to* ANGELO, *who has picked a leaflet up*]: What's it all about?

ANGELO [*thrilling with exaltation, as though what he read was for him an article of faith*]: Oggi: Cinema Reale: grande rappresentazione! . . . Saffo—Gli Amanti di Mitelene.

ADRIAN [*with a gesture of impatience*]: Oh, throw it away.

ANGELO [*perusing still, his whole face alight*]: La Bella Courtezan . . . La Pompadour . . . Una Assassina d'Amore . . . La Vita di Londra . . .

ADRIAN [*with the pram moving towards the house, followed by* ERIC *and* LORD ORKISH]: By the by, I don't even know my child's name!

ERIC: He gives me the impression rather of *an Hermione* . . .

ADRIAN: Hermione? Nonsense, Eric. He has an air of Claud. Or Gervase even.

ERIC: Gervase?

ADRIAN [*to baby*]: Hello, Gervase!

LORD ORKISH [*prosaically*]: His name's Charles.

ADRIAN [*disappointed*]: Charles!

LORD ORKISH: Charles Augustus Frederic Humphrey Percy Sydney.

ADRIAN: I intend calling my son *Gervase*.

ERIC: Why not Gerry?

ADRIAN: No; Gervase.

ERIC: Gerry!

[*Exeunt, Gerrying and Gervaseing one another to house.*]

ANGELO [*still perusing the leaflet, dawdling, in tones of sheerest ecstasy and joy*]: La Pompadour . . . La Vita-Dollar. . . .

Looking like some statue of Verrocchio, he raises his arms yearningly, murmuring, "Dollar!" "Dollar!" "La Vita-Dollar!'

as

THE CURTAIN FALLS

A Note on the Texts

The typescript of *The Mauve Tower* is held by Rhees Library, University of Rochester, and is annotated in Firbank's hand "Not to publish!" on its title page. The typescript of *A Disciple from the Country* is held by the Rare Book and Manuscript Library of Columbia University and is similarly annotated "Not to be published!" The texts printed here (which I first edited from the typescripts for *The Early Firbank*) retain most of Firbank's eccentricities regarding capitalization and punctuation; a few errors in grammar and spelling have been silently corrected—as they no doubt would have been had these plays been prepared for publication in his lifetime.

No manuscript or typescript survives for *The Princess Zoubaroff*. The text presented here is essentially that of the first edition (Grant Richards, 1920), with some corrections. When Duckworth & Company (London) reprinted the play in *The Complete Ronald Firbank* (1961), they made numerous minor changes, without explanation or authorization: they (the editor or editors responsible are not named) lower-cased some of Firbank's capitals (but inconsistently), added several commas, deleted many others, changed some of his semi-colons to commas and some of his exclamation points to question marks (and vice versa), corrected most of the errors in place-names and in French words (but only a few of those in Italian), and in a few cases altered Firbank's syntax or wording. (For example, they "corrected" Monsignor Vanhove's quotation from the Gospels in act 2, scene 16, but since it's as likely that the Monsignor is merely paraphrasing, if not improvising, I've restored the first edition's wording. And where the first edition has the Nurse say, at the beginning of act 3, "It's quiet enough, it's true, now the mistress has gone," Duckworth has her say

"It's queer enough . . ."—which may indeed be the case in the context of the play, but which is certainly an unwarranted change.)

I have ignored most of these changes and kept only the bona fide corrections to the place-names (like Pala d'Oro for the first edition's Pallo d'Oro), foreign words (with further corrections to the Italian taken from Brophy's *Prancing Novelist* and from Italian Firbank scholar Fabio Cleto), and only those of Duckworth's commas that struck me as absolutely necessary for clarity. I have eliminated some of Firbank's hyphens (to-morrow, Great-Dane, wedding-ring) and aimed for a certain consistency in some words; for example, Calvary is capitalized in one place but not in another; since Firbank seemed to prefer a capitalized Calvary elsewhere—as in his novel *Caprice*—I've consistently capitalized the word.

If anything, my editing has been too conservative, too respectful of a first edition that, although proofread by Firbank, does not seem to have been professionally copy-edited. Aberrant spellings and unusual capitalization and punctuation can be expressive, even entertaining, so I've retained as many of these as possible (in all three plays); but where they seemed to be the result of carelessness on Firbank's part (and/or negligent copy-editing on Grant Richards's part), I have followed Duckworth's lead and normalized them. Consequently, Reggie speaks here (on p. 114 as he did on p. 754 of *The Complete Firbank*) of "A Iokanaan" rather than of "An 'Iaokannan' " (as he did on p. 95 of the first edition); he is referring to the John the Baptist character in Wilde's *Salomé,* where the name is spelled Iokanaan in the French edition—Jokannan in the English translation—so there seemed no point in retaining Firbank's bizarre, impossible spelling since Wilde's is what he was obviously groping after. If this were a scholarly edition of Firbank's plays, all such changes would be listed here; but as this is a trade edition intended for the general reader—who is unlikely to be interested, for example, that Firbank spelled "edelweiss" as "Eidelweiss," nor that I've compromised in this instance by correcting the spelling but retaining the capital E (since he preferred to capitalize the names of flowers)—I've decided against such scholarly apparatus. That can wait until the happy day when a definitive, scholarly edition of Firbank's complete works is possible.